Spreadsheets for Business Students

An Active Learning Approach

for Lotus 1-2-3 release 2.0 and later; VP-Planner and VP-Planner Plus; As-Easy-As

Colston West

The author is a member of Bristol Business School, and has varied experience in industry and commerce, in addition to consultancy, business education and training

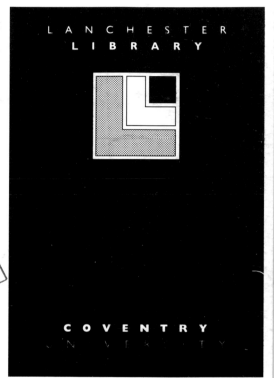

DP PUBLICATIONS LIMITED
Aldine Place
142/144 Uxbridge Road
London W12 8AW
1991

Acknowledgements

My thanks are due to the following:

Mike Bendrey and Roger Hussey for permission to use examples from our book: *ACCOUNTING AND FINANCE FOR BUSINESS STUDENTS* (*DP Publications*)

The many students in the Bristol Business School who used the experimental booklet which preceded this book, and to Kate, Molly and Nick who tried out various sessions of this book, for their time, patience, helpful comments and criticisms.

A CIP record for this book is available from the British Library

ISBN 1 870941 83 7
Copyright Colston West © 1991
Reprinted 1992 (with corrections)

Pageset by
   Kai, 21 Sycamore Rise,
   Cinderhill, Nottingham

Printed in Great Britain by
   The Guernsey Press Co Ltd,
   Guernsey, Channel Islands

Contents

Contents

Preface

1. Who should use this book?

This book has been designed for students on any course where acquaintance with the basics of spreadsheets is required. It requires very little (if any) input by the lecturer, and can be used on any machine/system with Lotus 1-2-3 version 2.0 (or above) or compatible spreadsheets (such as VP-Planner and As-Easy-As).

The examples have a business emphasis, and many have been taken from *Accounting & Finance for Business Students* by Bendrey, Hussey and West (*DP Publications*). However, it must be emphasised that this present book can be used quite independently, since all the examples are given in full.

A lecturers' supplement disk is available free to *bona fide* lecturers who adopt the book as a course text. See paragraph 8 of this Preface for details.

2. The nature of the book

This is *not* a traditional manual or text-book.

The author has found that students learn little or nothing from lectures about spreadsheets, however well-presented. There are many manuals available for spreadsheets, particularly Lotus 1-2-3, and although these are mostly excellent and comprehensive, they are also often too expensive and too forbidding to be recommended to students starting to learn the basics of spreadsheets on their own.

The author experimented with a 24-page A4 'teach yourself'-type booklet which was issued free to students on HND, foundation and first-year degree courses. This has proved remarkably successful over the last few years.

This present book is an expansion of this booklet, which 'gets you cracking' straightaway. There are no boring introductory chapters explaining Function Keys and Tree Diagrams of Subcommands and what-have-you. These aspects are introduced gradually in the course of the sessions and are summarised in the appendices.

3. The scope of the book

A book of this size cannot be completely comprehensive. That is the function of the manuals and the £20 popular guides. Students can progress to these when they have overcome their apprehensions with the aid of this 'getting started' book. The idea is to give students confidence in the basics of:

- ❑ constructing spreadsheet models;
- ❑ saving and retrieving files;
- ❑ graphing;
- ❑ printing spreadsheets and graphs;
- ❑ using a spreadsheet as a database;
- ❑ creating and using macros.

4. The layout of the book

The book contains ten sessions, most of them containing work and instruction which should take the average student not more than an hour or so at the computer or computer terminal. If a student finds that a session is taking longer than the time available, instructions are given early in the course on how to save and retrieve the work already covered.

Each session usually has the following design:

❏ objectives of the session;

❏ instructions and explanation;

❏ summary of the session;

❏ activities for further practice;

❏ an objective test.

These ten sessions are followed by three practice sessions, in which students are invited to solve problems in simple management accounting topics by setting out the data on a worksheet and designing a format to solve the problem. Guidance is provided, and solutions are explained and illustrated.

5. Effective use of the book

○ *By students on a taught course*

  ➪ Your lecturer will advise you which sessions to practise and when.

  ➪ Work through the instructions and explanations *slowly* and *carefully*.

  ➪ Remember that you are learning by doing.

  ➪ Each time you do something, watch what happens on the screen, ask yourself why, and read the explanation.

○ *By lecturers on a taught course*

  ➪ The first few sessions can be set early in the course, so that students can gain confidence.

  ➪ Subsequent sessions can be set in accordance with the requirements of the course. For example, the sessions on cash flow forecasts could be set several weeks before an assignment which required the preparation of a cash flow forecast.

  ➪ The objective tests could be used at tutorials, allowing, say, two minutes for the students to make their choice, and then asking a particular student to explain his/her choice.

  ➪ Activities could be suggested or set, depending on the time available.

○ *By students studying independently*

  ➪ Follow the suggestions above for students on a taught course.

  ➪ Answers to the objective tests are given at the end of this book.

  ➪ If you have difficulty with any of the activities suggested at the end of each session, repeat the session again, slowly and carefully.

6. Note on spreadsheets

This book uses **Lotus 1-2-3** version 2.0 or 2.01. It was tempting to use later versions such as 2.2, 3.0 or 3.1, but although these contain some improvements and enhancements, students might find it annoying if keystrokes in the text did not work. In any case, later versions have retained the keystrokes of version 2, and this book is intended to teach the basic skills. Printing with **ALLWAYS** (provided with version 2.2) is more sophisticated than 'ordinary' printing, but I feel that 'ordinary' skills should precede the more sophisticated ones.

Compatible spreadsheets, such as **VP-Planner** (and **VP-Planner Plus**) and **As-Easy-As** are in common use. There are some minor differences between them and **Lotus 1-2-3**, and I have attempted to point out the differences particularly in the early stages of the book to help students who might otherwise get confused. Minor differences, for example the use of *General* for *Global*, are ignored, since the keystroke G is the same. Also the messages in the control panel are quoted for **Lotus 1-2-3**; the messages given by the other programs quite often have different wording, but the same intent, and to have quoted all the variants would be tedious for the reader. However, wherever the actual keystrokes are different (and this applies particularly to **As-Easy-As**) and also where a different procedure is required, the instructions are given in full for each particular program. The reader should note the references for the program being used as set out in *Conventions used in this book* which follows.

7. Conventions used in this book

term	meaning
{123}	Instructions specific to **Lotus 1-2-3**
{VP}	Instructions specific to **VP-Planner** and **VP-Planner Plus**
{VPP}	Instructions specific to **VP-Planner Plus**
{AEA}	Instructions specific to **As-Easy-As, version 4.00Q** (Earlier versions may lack some features described in this book. These variations, where known, are noted in the text at points where they might cause confusion.)
Press <Esc>	Press the key marked 'Esc'
Press <Ctrl>+<Break>	Press and hold down the key marked 'Ctrl', and press the 'Break' key. Then release the 'Ctrl' key
Press /wey or /WEY	Press the keys as indicated, ignoring uppercase or lowercase. In Session 1, lowercase is shown for clarity, but uppercase from Session 2 onwards. See note in Session 2, paragraph 3
Type Total	Type the letters shown in bold type, in this case 'Total'
[range]	Specify a range by typing it in, or pointing, as described in Session 3
AFBIS	*Accounting and Finance for Business Students*: Reference to examples in *Accounting and Finance for Business Students* by **Bendrey, Hussey and West** (*DP Publications*) are to chapter and paragraph numbers. (See paragraph 1 of this Preface)

8. Free lecturers' supplement

The lecturers' supplement is a copyright-free $5\frac{1}{4}''$ (360K) PC-compatible disk, incorporating files for the models in the book. Files are in .WKS and WK1 format suitable for all four programs (123, VP, VPP, AEA). This disk is available free from the publishers to bona fide lecturers who wish to adopt the book as a course text.

9. Note concerning this 1992 reprint

This reprint incorporates minor amendments to the text of the 1991 first edition; these are mainly corrections of misprints and minor additions resulting from the suggestions of lecturers and students, to whom the author is indebted.

SESSION 1
Getting Started

1. Objectives

At the end of this session, you will be able to:

- ❏ load a blank worksheet (**Lotus 1-2-3, VP-Planner, VP-Planner Plus** or **As-Easy-As**);
- ❏ enter names into cells;
- ❏ correct your typing before entry into a cell;
- ❏ edit your typing after entry into a cell;
- ❏ move the cursor around the screen;
- ❏ understand <ESCAPE>, the panic button;
- ❏ end the session correctly.

2. Introduction

This book is intended for students who want to learn the basics of spreadsheets.

Many students look at a blank spreadsheet and wonder what on earth to do next. This book tells you what to do next.

You will be instructed what key to press and then told what should have happened on the screen, and why.

> **Advice**
> - ○ Work initially at a very slow pace.
> - ○ Follow the instructions carefully.
> - ○ Inspect the screen after each single keystroke.
> - ○ Ask yourself 'What has changed?'.
> - ○ Ask yourself 'What did the keystroke achieve?'.

If you go too fast, you will learn little and get into a mess. But don't worry if you do get in a mess: you will be shown how to get out of it.

Throughout this book, **Lotus 1-2-3** is used. If you are using **VP-Planner** or **VP-Planner Plus** or **As-Easy-As**, you may occasionally have to use slightly different keystrokes. In the early stages at least you will be told what to do when differences between the design of spreadsheets arise. For example, instructions specific to **VP-Planner** will be indicated like this: {VP}. See *Conventions used in this book* preceding this Session.

Before we start, you need to have a blank spreadsheet on the screen before you.

If you have already got that far, skip to paragraph 6. *The screen.*

If you have not, read one of the following sections, 3. *If you have a hard disk,* 4. *If you have no hard disk* or 5. *If you are at a college or polytechnic.*

3. If you have a hard disk

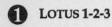 LOTUS 1-2-3

When you see the command prompt **C>** or **C:\>**,

type | cd\123 | Press <Enter>

This should switch you to the directory in which Lotus 1-2-3 is installed. 'CD' stands for 'Change Directory'. Note particularly the backslash \ is *not* a forward slash /.

You should get a prompt **C>** or **C:\123>**.

If you get a message on the screen 'Invalid Directory', Lotus 1-2-3 may have been installed in another directory. For example the directory may be called 'Lotus', in which case, you would have to

type | cd\lotus | Press <Enter>

To find the name of the directory, you could, at the **C>** prompt,

type | dir/p | Press <Enter>

and look for a likely name against the <DIR> entries.

When you have succeeded,

type | lotus | Press <Enter>

☞ You will see on the screen the Lotus Access System Screen.

Read what it says.

Since we want a 1-2-3 empty spreadsheet, make sure that the menu pointer (the highlight bar at the top of the screen) is over 1-2-3. If it is not (eg if you have accidentally moved the pointer with the right or left arrow keys to highlight one of the other items on the top line), move the pointer back to 1-2-3, using the arrow keys.

> *Tip:* If the arrow keys do not work and you hear a 'beep', you are using a keyboard which combines the numeric keypad with the arrow keys. Press <Num Lock> to change the keys back to being arrow keys. <Num Lock> is a 'toggle' between the two modes. The Access Screen will show Press [NUM LOCK] at the bottom of the screen if <Num Lock> is on. Pressing <Num Lock> turns it off.

② VP-PLANNER

The program is probably installed in a directory called VP or VPP. See the instructions for 1-2-3 above to find the name of the directory.

Type `cd\vp` (or whatever the directory is called). Press <Enter>

The prompt will be **C>** or **C:\VP>** or similar.

Type `vp` Press <Enter>

☞ The VP-Planner Access System Screen will appear.

Make sure the menu pointer (the highlighted rectangle) is over

`1. Worksheet only`

and Press <Enter>

The blank worksheet should appear.

② VP-PLANNER PLUS

The program is probably installed in a directory called VPP.

Type `cd\vpp` Press <Enter>

[If this does not work, follow the instructions under 1-2-3 above for finding the name of the directory.]

At the prompt **C>** or **C:\VPP>** or similar

Type `vpp` Press <Enter>

☞ An introductory screen with a copyright message will appear, then a blank spreadsheet with the same message.

Press <Enter>

The worksheet loses the message and becomes blank.

③ AS-EASY-AS

The program is probably installed in a directory called "Aseasy".

Type `cd\aseasy` Press <Enter>

[If this does not work, follow the instructions under 1-2-3 above for finding the name of the directory.]

At the prompt **C>** or **C:\ASEASY>**,

Type `aseasy` Press <Enter>

☞ The program will load and a screen full of information will appear. ...

Press any key.

A blank worksheet will appear, but possibly with a message.

To get rid of the message,

Type [/wey]

Don't worry about what happens on the screen while you are typing /wey. You will understand in time!

The message will disappear, and you will be left with a blank worksheet.

4. If you have no hard disk

1. Start you computer as usual with the DOS disk

2. Wait for the A> prompt

3. Remove the DOS disk

4. Insert your system disk

5. Type A: Press <Enter> to make sure drive A is the current drive

6. Type lotus or vp or vpp or aseasy

7. Press <Enter>

8. Follow the directions in paragraph 3 above, from the point marked ☞ in the section for your particular spreadsheet program.

5. If you are at a college or polytechnic

The terminal may be "networked".

The procedures vary, and instructions are probably on the machine.

A typical procedure might be:

1. Turn on the machine

2. Follow the instructions on the screen

Typical instructions might be:

a. Choose UTILITIES to FORMAT your floppy disk

b. Choose APPLICATIONS (move the menu bar to APPLICATIONS on the screen using the arrow keys on the keyboard and press <Enter>

c. Choose SPREADSHEETS

d. Choose the spreadsheet as available and required.

6. The screen

You should now have a blank worksheet on your screen.

There is a HORIZONTAL BORDER containing a one or two letter name for each COLUMN of the worksheet. Columns A to H are visible.

There is a VERTICAL BORDER containing a NUMBER for each ROW of the worksheet. Numbers 1-20 are visible.

There is also a CONTROL PANEL of 3 or 4 lines at the top or bottom of the screen (depending on the spreadsheet version).

Cell A1 should be highlighted sometimes with a blinking cursor.

In the control panel (on the left-hand side), A1 or A1: confirms that the cursor is on cell A1 of the worksheet.

Also in the control panel, there is a MENU INDICATOR which shows READY.

{123}   shows READY in the top right-hand corner.

{VP} and {VPP} show READY in the bottom right-hand corner.

{AEA}   shows READY at the top centre.

7. Entering names into cells

Type | Nebuchadnezzar | Press <Enter>

The name now appears in cell A1 on the worksheet.

I chose this name because it is difficult to spell!

If you made a mistake when typing it, leave the mistake for the moment. Your version, whether correct or incorrect, should be in the CONTROL PANEL, and if you look carefully, you will see that it is preceded by an apostrophe ('). I'll explain about this in due course.

You will notice that some of the letters spill over into cell B1. This is because, at present, each cell contains room for only 9 letters. Count the letters in cell A1 to check this. The fact that Nebuchadnezzar spills over into cell B1 does not matter, unless to want to type something into cell B1.

Suppose you typed Nebuchadnezzar incorrectly.

There are several ways to make a correction:

(a)   Type | Nebuchadnezzar | again. Press <Enter>

   The new entry replaces the old one in cell A1.

(b)   EDIT the present contents of the cell.

   Press | <F2> |

<F2> is the function key on the top or left-hand side of the keyboard.

8. Editing a cell entry

Note what happened when you pressed <F2>.

The MODE INDICATOR has chenged to EDIT, and 'Nebuchadnezzar' appears again in the second line of the control panel, ready for editing.

In EDIT mode, the following keys can be used:

Cursor Movement

Left arrow	Cursor moves one character to the left
Right arrow	Cursor moves one character to the right
<Shift>+<Tab>*	Cursor moves 5 {AEA:8} characters to left
<Tab>*	Cursor moves 5 {AEA:8} characters to right
<Home>	Cursor moves to the first character
<End>	Cursor moves to the last character

* The <Tab> key is sometimes marked with two arrows facing in opposite directions with a bar at the arrowhead.

Deleting Characters

<← del>*	Deletes the character to left of cursor
<Del>*	Deletes the character at cursor position

* The <← del> key is the key with a left facing arrow, usually above the <Enter> key. The <Del> key is usually marked 'Del', and can found near the bottom right-hand corner of the keyboard.

Inserting Characters

There are two ways to insert characters:

(a) Insert Mode

Place the cursor over the character AFTER the position where you wish to insert a character. For example, if you wish to insert a 't' into 'Lous' to make 'Lotus', place the cursor over the 'u' and type 't'.

(b) Replace or Overtype Mode

Press the <Ins> key once.

[Note: {123,AEA} OVR appears at foot of screen

{VP,VPP} blinking cursor size reduces to underline]

6

Place the cursor over the character you wish to replace. For example, if you wish to replace the 'b' in 'Lobus' to make 'Lotus', place the cursor over the 'b' and type 't'.

Note that the <Ins> key is a 'toggle-switch' (i.e. it changes to and fro) between Insert and Replace modes. Usually Insert mode is the more useful, and it is probably best to keep the toggle in Insert mode.

While you are in Edit mode, practise with some of the above keystrokes, altering Nebuchadnezzar as many times as you want.

When he is spelt correctly, press <Enter> to transfer him to cell A1, and return to READY mode.

9. Moving the cursor

Now for some more practice.

I assume the cursor is still on cell A1. If it is not,

Press | <Home> |

which returns the cursor to cell A1.

Press | <↓> | (down-arrow) once.

The cursor moves to cell A2.

Press | <↓> | | <↓> | | <→> | | <→> |

The cursor should now be in cell C4.

Press | <F5> | Type | a5 | Press | <Enter> |

The cursor moves to cell A5. <F5> is the 'GoTo' key. Follow it with any cell reference, and the cursor will go there.

With the cursor on cell A5,

Type | Shadrach | Press | <↓> |

Note that you have pressed the down-arrow instead of <Enter>.

'Shadrach' appears in cell A5, and the cursor moves to cell A6, i.e. one cell in the direction of the down-arrow.

Type | Meshach | Press | <↓> |

'Meshach' appears in cell A6 and the cursor moves to cell A7.

Type | Abednego | Press | <→> |

'Abednego' appears in cell A7 and the cursor moves to cell B7.

If you have mis-spelt any of the names, try correcting them with the <F2> Edit key, as described above.

10. Altering an entry before pressing <Enter> or an arrow key

Move the cursor to cell A8.

Type | `Belteshassar` | BUT DO NOT PRESS <Enter>.

You should have typed 'Belteshazzar', i.e. zz instead of ss.

You can use the <← del> key or the <Del> keys to erase the last characters typed.

Press | `<← del>` | four times

This erases 'ssar'.

Type | `zzar` |

'Belteshazzar' is now ready for entry into cell A8.

Alternatively, you could have pressed <Esc> (before pressing <Enter>, but this would have wiped out the whole of 'Belteshassar', and then you would have had to type 'Belteshazzar' in full.

11. <ESCAPE> – The panic button

Sometimes you find that you have 'got in a mess', and things appear on the screen that you do not understand, due, perhaps, to pressing the wrong keys.

If this happens, pressing <Esc> will usually get you back to the READY mode. You may have to press <Esc> more than once.

Try this:

Press | `/ w g f` |

What to do next?   You don't know yet?

Press | `<Esc>` | four times, and you are back where youstarted!

Now: {123, VP, VPP only}

Press | `/ w g f` | again.

Press | `<Ctrl>+<Break>` |

and again you are back where you started, in READY mode.

<Ctrl>+<Break> has the effect of pressing <Esc> innumerable times.

8

12. Before you end this session

You may be wondering about a number of things:

How do you 'blank out' a cell easily?

How do you alter the width of a column?

How do you clear the whole worksheet of the names you have been entering?

How do you move quickly to other parts of the worksheet?

How big is your total worksheet?

Why have I only let you enter names so far?

How do you save the data you have entered on the worksheet?

Where will it all end?

All these questions (apart from the last one) will be answered in the following sessions. Be patient!

Unless you have time or inclination to carry out the following activity, you can finish this session:

Press [/   ]

Note that this is the </> key, NOT the <\> key.

The main menu will appear in the control panel or as a drop-down menu.

Move the cursor to QUIT or EXIT and press <Enter>

Then:

{123} and {AEA}	Move the cursor to 'Yes' and press <Enter>
	If you returned to the Access screen,
	Choose 'Exit' with the cursor and press <Enter>
{VP} and {VPP}	Type 'Y' for Yes
{VP only}	Move cursor to 'Quit' and press <Enter>

You should now be back at the DOS prompt C> or C:\123 or whatever the directory is called. Park your hard disc if necessary.

If you are on a network system, you should be at the menu screen, in which case press <Esc> to go back through the menus and then follow the instructions on the screen.

Note that we are losing all the names we have been using for practice in this session, and we shall start the next session with a blank worksheet.

13. Summary

In this session you should have achieved the objectives set out at the start of this session.

In particular, you have become acquainted with:

`</>`		the MENU key
`<F2>`		the EDIT key
`<F5>`		the GOTO key
`<Esc>`		the PANIC button
`<Ctrl>+<Break>`		the multiple <Esc> keys
`<Home>`	in READY mode	the return to cell A1 key
`<Home>`	in EDIT mode	the return to first character key
`<End>`	in EDIT mode	the move to last character key
`<Ins>`		the Insert or Replace toggle.

14. Activity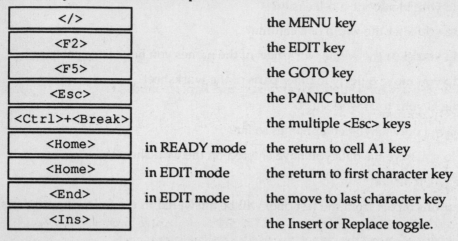

Move the cursor to any blank cell and practise entering names (not numbers). Make deliberate mistakes in your typing, and correct them

(a) before pressing <Enter>, and

(b) after pressing <Enter>, i.e using the <F2> Edit key.

15. Objective test ☐ A ☐ B ☑ C ☐ D

1. When first loaded, a blank worksheet shows columns A-H. Each column has a (default) column-width of

    ☐ A 7 characters

    ☐ B 8 characters

    ☐ C 9 characters

    ☐ D 10 characters

2. In order to edit an entry in a cell, the edit key to press is

    ☐ A <Enter>

    ☐ B <F2>

    ☐ C <F3>

    ☐ D <F5>

10

3. In edit mode, the key to press to move the cursor to the first character is

    ☐ A <Tab>

    ☐ B <Shift>+<Tab>

    ☐ C <End>

    ☐ D <Home>

4. In edit mode, the key to toggle between Insert and Replace modes is

    ☐ A <Num Lock>

    ☐ B <Del>

    ☐ C <Ins>

    ☐ D <Esc>

5. If you are ready to make an entry into cell D4, and you want to press the key which will make the entry and move the cursor to cell E5, the key to press is

    ☐ A <→>

    ☐ B <↓>

    ☐ C <F5>

    ☐ D none of these

6. The <Goto> key is

    ☐ A <F2>

    ☐ B <F3>

    ☐ C <F4>

    ☐ D <F5>

7. If you have "got lost" after pressing **/ R F F**, and you don't know what to do, you can get back to the READY mode by pressing

    ☐ A <Esc> four times

    ☐ B <Ctrl>+<Ins>

    ☐ C <Enter> three times

    ☐ D none of these

8. The cursor is in cell B2, and you wish to move it to cell C5. The least number of key-presses to achieve this is

    ☐ A <→><→><→><↓>

    ☐ B <F5><c><5><Enter>

    ☐ C <→><↓><↓>

    ☐ D <↓><↓><→>

9. You want to enter 'Daniel' into a cell. You have typed 'Saniel', and realise you have made a mistake, but have not yet pressed <Enter>. The quickest way to correct this is to

    ☐ A press <Esc> and type 'Daniel'

    ☐ B press <Home>, then <Ins> to get into replace mode, and then type 'Daniel"

    ☐ C press <←del> 6 times, and type 'Daniel'

    ☐ D none of these

10. You need a cup of coffee, and you want to leave your worksheet and the spreadsheet program, without saving any of your entries. The first key to press is

    ☐ A </>

    ☐ B <\>

    ☐ C <Esc>

    ☐ D <Home>

SESSION 2
A Simple Worksheet

1. Objectives

At the end of this session, you will be able to:

- ❏ appreciate what a worksheet looks like
- ❏ enter more labels into a worksheet
- ❏ align labels to the left, right and centre of a cell
- ❏ use the GoTo (F5) key to move around the worksheet
- ❏ widen a column from the default width
- ❏ make dotted lines using the repeat key (\)
- ❏ copy cells, including pointing with the cursor
- ❏ clear a cell completely
- ❏ enter values into cells
- ❏ enter formulae into cells
- ❏ copy formulae into other cells
- ❏ save a new worksheet to disk
- ❏ save an updated worksheet to disk
- ❏ change data entries and observe the effect on related cells containing formulae.

2. Introduction

In this session you will create a worksheet containing some simple VAT calculations. You will learn some new skills as you do so.

The worksheet you will create looks something like the table on the following page.

L. Marshfield   **VAT Calculations**
                      Description of Items

	Boxes	@ per box	Amount	VAT @ 15%	Total
	No.	£	£	£	£
Sale	50	12	600	90	690
Purchase	50	10	500	75	575

Summary:	£
Output tax =	90
Input tax =	75

[Note: This table is taken from AFBIS, chapter entitled *Deductions from Pay and Value Added Tax*.]

3. Entering the labels

LABELS include words such as Nebuchadnezzar. You may remember from Session 1 that when you entered his name into a cell, an apostrophe (') appeared before his name in the Control Panel.

This apostrophe is the DEFAULT LABEL PREFIX, and will appear in the Control Panel if your cell entry starts with a letter (as distinct from a number or one of the special numeric symbols which we shall describe later on).

DEFAULT means that the program inserts this for you unless you do something specific to the contrary.

LABEL PREFIX is a symbol placed before the label, telling the program how you want the label to appear in the cell.

In this case, the apostrophe tells the program that you wish the label to appear in the cell *left-aligned*, i.e. with the left-hand letter flush with the left-hand side of the cell.

Start this session with a blank worksheet, as you learnt in Session 1.

If you still have some entries in your worksheet, you can clear them by typing / W E Y (/ Worksheet Erase Yes). I am assuming that you do not want to preserve these entries, because /WEY loses them unless you have already saved the worksheet. Later on in this session, you will learn how to save a worksheet.

[Note: From this point onwards, in the interest of consistency, commands such as /WEY are printed in uppercase (CAPITALS). However, you do not need to press <Shift>+w, for example, for the W of /WEY. Command letters can be pressed in either uppercase or lowercase, so simply press the key shown; it does not matter if <Caps Lock> has been activated. To continue to print /WEY as /wey might prove irritating, since W stands for Worksheet, E stands for Erase and Y for Yes, as shown in the control panel.]

Press [<Home>] if your cursor is not in cell A1.

Type <u>L. Marshfield</u> <Enter>

L. Marshfield will appear in cell A1, and A1: 'L. Marshfield will appear in the Control Panel.

Note the apostrophe before the label in the Control Panel, indicating that the label is left-aligned.

Now enter some more labels, as follows:

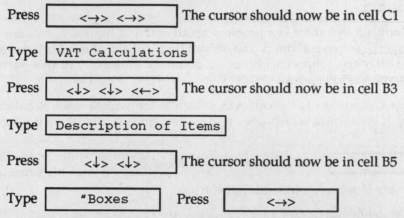

Press <→> <→> The cursor should now be in cell C1

Type VAT Calculations

Press <↓> <↓> <←> The cursor should now be in cell B3

Type Description of Items

Press <↓> <↓> The cursor should now be in cell B5

Type "Boxes Press <→>

Note that you typed ``Boxes. The inverted comma (``) is a label prefix which right-aligns the label in the cell.

The cursor should now be in cell C5.

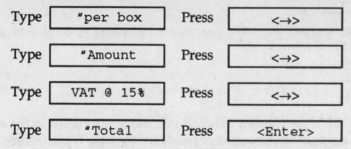

Type "per box Press <→>

Type "Amount Press <→>

Type VAT @ 15% Press <→>

Type "Total Press <Enter>

The cursor should be positioned over the last entry in cell F5.

Note that *per box*, *Amount* and *Total* are right-aligned in the cells. The other label VAT @ 15% is exactly 9 characters, and therefore fills the default cell-width of 9 characters.

Press <f5> a8 <Enter>

<F5> is the GoTo key, and the cursor should now be in cell A8.

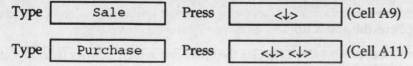

Type Sale Press <↓> (Cell A9)

Type Purchase Press <↓> <↓> (Cell A11)

15

Type | `^Summary:` | Press | `<↓> <↓>` | (Cell A13)

Note: the caret (^) is a label-prefix which centres the label.

Type | `Output tax =` | Press | `<↓>` | (Cell A14)

Type | `Input tax =` | Press | `<Enter>` | (Cell A14)

4. Widening a column

You have probably noticed that there is a problem about entering figures in column B: the labels in column A overflow into column B. The default width of all columns is 9 characters, and it is possible to alter the column width of all columns. However, in this particular worksheet, only column A is too narrow.

Place the cursor over Output tax =, i.e. cell A13, which is the widest label in column A, apart from the label *L. Marshfield* which does not matter, since it overflows into cell B2, which is empty.

Press | `/ W C S` | (/ Worksheet Column Set-width)

The Control Panel reads Enter column width (1..240): 9

({AEA} reads Enter Column Width (1..72) ? 9)

You could type the number 12, and press <Enter> which would widen the column to cover all of Output tax =. However, try this:

Press | `<→> <→> <→>`

The cursor should now cover Output tax = (12 characters including spaces), and the 9 should have changed to 12 in the Control Panel.

Press | `<Enter>`

and column A now has a width of 12.

[For {123}{AEA}, note the [W12] in the Control Panel. If you move the cursor to the other columns, this message does not appear for columns of the default width. Try it and see.]

5. Making dotted lines

Now you need some dotted lines. You could type them in as a row of hyphens, but here is a short-cut.

Move the cursor to cell A10

Type | `\-` | <Enter>

A row of twelve hyphens fills cell A10.

The backslash (\) is a label prefix which repeats the character which follows it, in this case a hyphen.

6. Copying cells

You need hyphens in cells B10 to F10 inclusive. You could repeat the technique in paragraph 5 for each of these cells. But there is an easier way.

Make sure the cursor is on cell A10.

Press `/ C` (/ Copy)

The Control Panel reads Enter range to copy FROM: A10..A10

A10..A10 means cell A10! (We shall look at larger ranges later.)

You want accept this cell as the cell to be copied, so

Press `<Enter>`

The Control Panel now reads Enter range to copy TO: A10.

A10 is given because that is where the cursor is.

The range you want to copy to is B10..F10.

Press `<→>` This moves the cursor to B10.

Press `.(a full stop!)`

This full stop ANCHORS the cursor which can now be extended to cell F10.

Press `<→> <→> <→> <→>`

The cursor should now cover cells B10, C10, D10, E10 and F10.

Press `<Enter>`

The hyphens should now extend from cells A10 to F10 inclusive. Move the cursor along this line. You will see from the Control Panel that each cell contains the repeating label \-.

Note: This method is known as Pointing with the cursor, i.e. moving the cursor over the range required after anchoring the cursor with a full stop. You could, instead, have typed in the range in after pressing /C<Enter>, i.e typed b10.f10 - a single full stop will suffice - and then pressed <Enter>. If you prefer this method in the future, by all means use it. However, POINTING with the cursor is probably safer: you can see the range on the screen, whereas it is easy to make a mistake in typing in the reference cells of the range.

You should now be able to put dotted lines (using \- and the / Copy command) into the following cells:

B4 to C4 inclusive

B6 to F6 inclusive

A12

7. More labels and copying

You need some headings on line 7.

Cell B7 needs No. right-aligned

Cells C7 to F7 inclusive need the £ sign, right-aligned.

You should now be able to enter these labels. Try it!

If you still find this difficult, here are the key-presses:

Move to cell B7

Press | `"No.` | | `<→>` | | `"£` | <Enter> | `/C` | <Enter>

| `<→>` | | `. (a full stop)` | | `<→>` | | `<→>` | <Enter>

8. Clearing a cell

It is unlikely that you have managed so far without making some mistakes in your key-presses. In session 1 you learnt how to correct mistakes, particularly by editing entries in cells.

Here is a way to clear a cell completely:

Move the cursor to cell A16.

Type | `Rubbish` | <Enter>

Press | `/RE` | <Enter>

Note that after pressing / Range Erase, the Control Panel reads *Enter range to erase: A16..A16*. By pressing <Enter>, you erase the range A16..A16, i.e. cell A16.

9. Entering values

Numbers are now needed in cells B8, B9, C8 and C9.

These numbers are values, as distinct from labels. When you perform the following keypresses, look at the mode indicator after you make each keystroke. A cell entry which starts with a letter is treated as a label, whereas a cell entry which starts with a number is treated as a value. If you wish to have a label which is in fact a number (e.g. the year 1991), you would have to use a label-prefix.

Move the cursor to cell B8.

Type | `50` | `<↓>` | `50` | `<→>` | `10` | `<↑>` | `12` | `<→>`

The cursor should now be on cell D8.

10. Entering formulae

The numbers in the remaining cells (refer to the worksheet in paragraph 2 of this session) can be calculated from the values which you entered in cells B8, B9, C8 and C9. You will therefore enter formulae into these cells, as follows:

With the cursor over cell D8,

Type | +b8*c8 | <Enter>

You have now typed in a formula which multiplies any data figure entered in cell B8 by any data figure entered in cell C8. The + sign before the b of b8 tells the program that it is not a label. The asterisk (*) is the multiplication symbol. Note that the figure 600 appears in the cell, whereas the formula appears in the control panel.

Move the cursor to cell E8.

Type | +d8*15% | <Enter>   [Not {AEA} early versions: see ** below.]

This formula multiplies the figure in cell D8 by 15%. You will note that the figure in cell E8 is 90, whereas the formula appears in the control panel as +D8*0.15. The program has converted 15% to 0.15, which is the same thing. You could, of course, have typed 0.15 instead of 15%, and this is necessary in early versions of {AEA}**.

Move the cursor to cell F8.

Type | +d8+e8 | <Enter>

This formula adds the figure in cell D8 and the figure in cell e8. Again you will see the result of the addition in cell F8 (690) and the formula in the control panel.

11. Copying formulae

The formulae you require for line 9 (cells D9, E9 and F9) are similar to those in line 8. You could type in the formulae, substituting a 9 for an 8 in each case, but there is a quicker way:

Move the cursor to cell D8.

Type | / C | | <→> | | <→> | | <Enter> | | <↓> | | . | | <→> | | <→> | | <Enter> |

Note the full stop to anchor the cursor when you get to Enter range to copy TO: D9 in the control panel.

What you have done is copy the formulae in cells D8, E8 and F8 into cells D9, E9 and F9, and the program has converted the formulae to make them relative to line 9 instead of line 8.

Check that the figures in cells D9, E9 and F9 are 500, 75 and 575 respectively.

Check the formulae in these cells and compare them with those in line 8 above by moving the cursor over them and looking at the formulae in the control panel.

12. Completing the worksheet

You need to enter cell references in cells B13 and B14 in the 'Summary' to complete the worksheet.

Move to cell B13.

Type | +e8 | | <↓> | | +e9 | | <Enter>

Cells B13 and B14 now show the same figures as cells E8 and E9 respectively.

13. Saving your worksheet

The worksheet is now complete. In paragraph 15, you can experiment with altering the data and seeing how the worksheet responds, before you end this session.

However, you may want to save your masterpiece in its present state, so that you can experiment with it on some future occasion.

At present (unless there has been a power-cut or some similar disaster) the worksheet is still only in the memory of the computer. In order to be able to recall it when next you turn the computer on, the worksheet must be saved to a disk - either the hard disk (usually drive C: or perhaps D:) or your floppy disk (usually drive A: or B:).

Type | / F S

The control panel shows a message: *Enter save file name:* (or similar message) followed, perhaps, by something like:

C:\123*.wk1   or   A:*.wks   or   B:*.wk1

depending on the program you are using.

The C:\, A:\ or B:\ indicate the drive to which your worksheet will be saved. In the case of drives A: or B:, you should ensure that you have a suitable formatted disk in the appropriate drive.

The 123\ (usually only for the hard disk, drive C:) is the subdirectory to which your file will be saved.

The *.wk1 or *.wks is a 'blank' for the file name. The file name consists of the name (which will replace the *) and the extension (.wk1 or .wks). The extension is supplied automatically by the program. You must choose the file name.

If you are happy that this is the place where you want your worksheet to be saved, simply

Type | VATCALCS | <Enter>

and your worksheet will be saved to disk with the name VATCALCS.

If the program does NOT indicate where it will save your file, or if the indicated location is NOT where you want to save it, you should FIRST follow the following procedures, depending on the program you are using. Although the procedures are similar in principle, the details vary.

If the program does NOT indicate where it will save your file,or if the indicated location is NOT where you want to save it, you should FIRST follow the following procedures, depending on the program you are using. Although the procedures are similar in principle, the details vary.

If you are using {123} or {VPP}:

> Either:

> Press | `<Esc>` | until the mode indicator shows READY.

> Type | `/`   `F`   `D` |

The message *Enter current directory:* or *Enter Path:* appears.

Press `<Enter>` to accept the directory shown, or type in the directory you require. For example if the directory shown is *C:\123* and you want to save to your floppy disk in drive A:,

> Type | `A:` | `<Enter>`

This means that whenever, during the current session, you save by pressing /FS, the directory shown will be what you want.

> Press | `/`   `F`   `S` |

> Type | `vatcalcs` | `<Enter>`

The worksheet will saved as VATCALCS.WK1 or VATCALCS.WKS

> Or:

After pressing /FS, (if the directory shown is not what you want), press `<Esc>` and then type in the full drive name, pathname i.e subdirectory name (if necessary) and then the name of the file,

> e.g. | `<Esc>` | `c:\123\vatcalcs` | `<Enter>` |

> or | `<Esc>` | `a:\vatcalcs` | `<Enter>` |

If you are using {VP} (Planner NOT Plus)

Pressing /FS produces the message *Enter File Name:* but this is not followed by any indication of the drive or path. However, a list appears in the second line of the control panel showing files (if any) which have previously been saved to the directory, and this may be sufficient clue for you.

To make sure which directory your present worksheet will be saved to,

> Press | `<Esc>` | three times to get back to READY

21

Type | A: | `<Enter>`

This means that whenever, during the current session, you save by pressing /FS, the directory will be what you want.

Press | /   F   S |

Type | vatcalcs | `<Enter>`

The worksheet will be saved as VATCALCS.WKS in the directory you specified.

If you are using {AEA}:

Pressing /FS produces the message *STORE:Name of file ?* followed by the flashing cursor inviting you to enter the filename. There is no indicaton of the drive or path. However, pressing `<Esc>` shows this information, together with a list of all files (if any) which have already been saved to the directory shown.

If this IS the directory to which you wish to save your worksheet,

Type | vatcalcs | `<Enter>`

If this is NOT the directory to which you wish to save your worksheet,

either:

type in the full drive name, pathname i.e subdirectory name (if necessary), and the the name of the file,

e.g. | c:\myfiles\vatcalcs | `<Enter>`

or | a:\vatcalcs | `<Enter>`

or:

press | `<Esc>` | | /   F   D |

and then, when you see the message *Directory is >>*, type in the directory you require, e.g. c:\myfiles or a: and then `<Enter>`

Then press | S (for Store) | | vatcalcs | `<Enter>`

The worksheet will be saved (stored) as VATCALCS.WKS in the directory you specified.

Note concerning Filenames

The file name can be up to eight characters long, followed by a full-stop and the 'extension' such as wk1 or wks. depending on which program you are using.

The eight characters of the file name can be letters (A-Z) or numbers (0-9) . Some other characters are acceptable, depending on the program you are using, but it is safer to keep to letters and or numbers, at least for the time being.

You can type the letters of the filename in small letters: the program will convert them to capitals.

14. Saving your worksheet again

If, in a session, you have already saved your worksheet and given it a name, and you wish, as is prudent, to save it from time to time to update your additions to it, you can repeat the /fs command.

Try this:

> Move the cursor on your VATCALCS worksheet to cell B12.

Type | `"£` | <Enter>

Type | `/ F S`

The control panel should read: *Enter save file name:* followed by the name that you previously gave to your worksheet file, i.e. VATCALCS.

Press | `<Enter>` | `R (Replace)`

The revised VATCALCS worksheet is now saved with the addition of your recent entry into cell B12.

15. Changing your data

Before you end this session, you may like to experiment with changing the data entered into cells B8, B9, C8 and C9.

For example, alter the figure in cell B8 to 100.

> Move the cursor to cell B8.

Type | `100` | <Enter>

The sale figures in cells D8, E8, F8 and B13 will have doubled.

Be careful not to type over the cells containing formulae. You will learn how to protect such cells from alteration in a later session.

When you have finished experimenting, you can end this session using the method described in session 1. Any changes to the data which you made in this paragraph will, of course, not be saved, unless you have used /FS again after the changes.

16. Summary

In this session you should have achieved the objectives set out at the start of this session.

In particular, you should have become acquainted with:

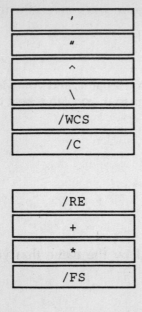

'	the left-align label prefix
"	the right-align label prefix
^	the centre label prefix
\	the repeat label prefix
/WCS	Worksheet Column Set-width
/C	the Copy command, including anchoring with a full-stop and pointing with the cursor
/RE	the Range Erase command
+	to precede a cell reference
*	the multiplication sign
/FS	the File Save command, and how to use it on first and subsequent occasions.

17. Activity

Create a worksheet from the following table:

Jean Landown	VAT Calculations		Net £	VAT(15%) £	Gross £
Sales:	20 bracelets @ £35 each		700	105	805
Purchases:	20 bracelets @ £20 each		400	60	460
Summary:	Output tax =	£105			
	Input tax =	£60			
Payable to HM Customs & Excise =		£45			

[Note: this table is taken from AFBIS, chapter entitled *Deductions from Pay and Value Added Tax*.]

You should try to convert this table to a format suitable for a worksheet, e.g. 'Bracelets' could be a heading for a column.

18. Objective test ☐ A ☐ B ☑ C ☐ D

1. The label prefix `` results in the label entered in a cell being
    ☐ A left aligned
    ☐ B right aligned
    ☐ C centred
    ☐ D repeated

2. If you enter no label prefix before a label, then the default is for the label to appear
    ☐ A left aligned
    ☐ B right aligned
    ☐ C centred
    ☐ D none of these

3. In order to widen a single column to a width of 12, the key presses are
    ☐ A /wcs12<Enter>
    ☐ B /rcs12<Enter>
    ☐ C \rcs12<Enter>
    ☐ D /wcs<Enter>12<Enter>

4. In order to make a row of hyphens entered in a cell, the key presses are
    ☐ A /-<Enter>
    ☐ B \-<Enter>
    ☐ C /\-<Enter>
    ☐ D - - - - - - - - -

5. In order to copy a row of hyphens from cell A7 to cells B7, C7 and D7, the key presses are, starting with the cursor over cell A7,
    ☐ A /C<→><→><→>.<Enter>
    ☐ B \C<→><→><→>.<Enter>
    ☐ C /C<Enter><→>.<→><→><Enter>

☐ D \C<Enter><→>.<→><→><Enter>

6. In order to clear cell A7 completely of its contents, the key presses, when the cursor is over cell A6, are

☐ A <→>\RE<Enter>

☐ B /RE<↓><Enter>

☐ C \REA7<Enter>

☐ D <↓>/RE<Enter>

7. If you wish to multiply the number 11 in cell A9 by the number 9 in cell B9, and obtain the result in cell C9, the formula to enter in cell C9 is

☐ A +a9xb9

☐ B +a9*b9

☐ C 11x9=

☐ D none of these

8. With the number 11 in cell A10 and the number 7 in cell B10, in order to obtain the product in cell C10, the way to copy the correct formula from cell C9 in question 7 above to cell C10 requires the following key presses, assuming the cursor is over cell C9:

☐ A /C<↓><Enter>

☐ B /C<Enter><↓><Enter>

☐ C <↓>/C<Enter><↑><Enter>

☐ D both B and C

9. For {123} and {VPP} users only:

You are saving a worksheet for the first time with the name BEDTIME. If when you press /FS, the control panel shows:

Enter save file name: C:\123\works*.wk1

in order to save your worksheet to a floppy disk in drive A:, you type:

☐ A bedtime<Esc>

☐ B <Esc><Esc>a\bedtime<Enter>

☐ C <Esc>a:bedtime<Enter>

☐ D <Esc><Esc>a:\bedtime<Enter>

9. For {VP} and {AEA} users only:

You are saving a worksheet for the first time with the name BEDTIME. If when you press /FS, the control panel shows:

Enter File Name: or STORE:Name of file ?,

in order to save your worksheet to a floppy disk in drive A:, you type:

☐ A bedtime<Esc>

☐ B <Esc><Esc>a\bedtime<Enter>

☐ C <Esc>a:/bedtime<Esc>

☐ D a:bedtime<Enter>

10. Assuming you have saved your worksheet BEDTIME correctly, and have made some additions which you now wish to save with it, under the same name, you should make the following key presses:

☐ A /FS<Enter>R

☐ B /FS<Enter><Enter>

☐ C /FSTeatime<Enter>

☐ D /FS<Enter>

SESSION 3
Bristol: Cash Flow Forecast

1. Objectives

At the end of this session, you will be able to:

- ❑ know the layout of a Cash Flow Forecast
- ❑ save a keystroke in copying to a range of cells
- ❑ widen a range of cells
- ❑ use the @SUM formula to total a range of cells
- ❑ practise saving the worksheet
- ❑ use pointing in entering a formula
- ❑ align a range of labels
- ❑ put commas into figures using /WGF
- ❑ translate a Cash Flow Forecast into a worksheet format

2. Introduction

In this session, you will create a worksheet containing a CASH FLOW FORECAST, and you will learn some more skills as you do so.

A Cash Flow Forecast is a financial statement of the cash expected to flow into and out of a business for a specified future period. The statement is usually presented as an analysis which shows detailed cash inflows at the top of the statement and detailed cash outflows below, with analysis columns for suitable periods of time, frequently months. At the foot of each column appears the balance of cash in hand expected at the end of the period to which the column relates. The purpose of the forecast is to aid cash planning and decision making. Control can be achieved by regular comparison of the planned cash flow with the actual flow. It is therefore a document which needs to be updated frequently, and its preparation in spreadsheet format enables this to be done more easily than with pencil and rubber or perhaps by re-typing.

'Cash' is usually taken to mean both cash-in-hand and cash-at-bank, i.e. money which is easily accessible.

3. Bristol: Cash Flow Forecast

The Cash Flow Forecast which you will be shown how to create on a worksheet is shown below. It is a personal cash flow forecast for a Mr. B. Bristol who expects to have savings in hand of £250 on 1st January, but knows that he must have £500 available by the end of June to be able to afford a holiday. The forecast shows his 'take-home' pay for the next six months, as well as his anticipated outgoings for the same period. The foot of each column shows his anticipated balance of cash at the end of each month.

[This example is taken from AFBIS, chapter entitled *Cash Planning and Personal Cash Flow*.]

	A	B	C	D	E	F	G	H
1	B. BRISTOL: CASH FLOW FORECAST							
2	for the six month period January - June							
3								
4	--							
5		JAN	FEB	MAR	APL	MAY	JUN	TOTAL
6		£	£	£	£	£	£	£
7	CASH INFLOWS							
8	Salary	700	700	700	700	700	700	4,200
9		---						
10	Total Inflows A	700	700	700	700	700	700	4,200
11	CASH OUTFLOWS:	===						
12	Rates				160			160
13	Rent	200	200	200	200	200	200	1,200
14	Electricity			180			180	360
15	Travel	50	50	50	50	50	50	300
16	Insurances	10	40	10	130	10	10	210
17	Sundries	120	120	120	120	120	120	720
18	Food	150	150	150	150	150	150	900
19	Holiday						500	500
20		---						
21	Total Outflows B	530	560	710	810	530	1,210	4,350
22		===						
23	NET CASH FLOW: A - B	170	140	(10)	(110)	170	(510)	(150)
24	Balances:							
25	Start of month	250	420	560	550	440	610	250
26	End of month	420	560	550	440	610	100	100
27	---------------------==							

Note: cells B25 and H25 = savings at 1st January

4. Approach

You could, of course, compose the worksheet in the same way as you entered VATCALCS in session 2, i.e. first labels, then values, and finally formulae.

However, in this session you will work down the worksheet more or less from top to bottom. i.e. a mixture of labels, values and formulae as you go. The idea is that once you get the hang of a principle, you may feel confident enough to make entries which are similar to previous entries on your own, without pressing or typing as instructed in detail. On the other hand, you may feel that you will learn more easily by carrying out the detailed instructions, and watching the screen carefully after each keystroke as suggested in session 1. The choice is yours! If you think you have made the wrong choice, you can always erase as much as you want and try the other method.

5. Entering the headings

Start this session with a blank worksheet, as you learnt in session 1.

Move the cursor to cell A1 (press Home if it is not already there).

Type | `B. BRISTOL: CASH FLOW FORECAST` | Press | `<Enter>` |

You will note that what you have typed now appears in cell A1, and that it spreads over into cells B1, C1 and D1. This does not matter, since you do not want to enter anything into those cells.

If you have made a typing error, you can either retype correctly, or use the <F2> edit key as you learnt in session 1, paragraph 8.

Press | `<↓>` | (Cell A2)

If you used <Caps Lock> for cell A1, turn it off now!

Type | `for the six month period January - June` |

Press | `<↓> <↓>` | (Cell A4)

Press | `\-` | Press <Enter>

This fills cell A4 with a line of hyphens.

Press | `/C` | <Enter>

This is the /Copy command.

Press | `<→>` | to move the cursor to cell B4

Type | `.(a full stop)` | to anchor the cursor

Move the cursor to cell H4 using the <→> key

Press | `<Enter>` |

This /Copy command should have copied the hyphens from cell A4 to cells B4 - H4 inclusive and the cursor should still be at cell A4.

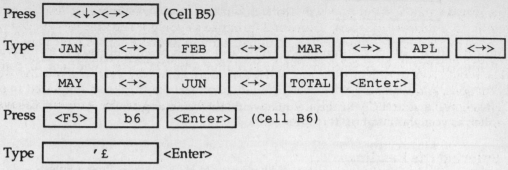

Press | `< ↓ >< → >` | (Cell B5)

Type | `JAN` | `< → >` | `FEB` | `< → >` | `MAR` | `< → >` | `APL` | `< → >`

| `MAY` | `< → >` | `JUN` | `< → >` | `TOTAL` | `<Enter>`

Press | `<F5>` | `b6` | `<Enter>` (Cell B6)

Type | `'£` | <Enter>

Note that a label prefix is necessary before the £ sign (except for {AEA}).

Type | `/C` | <Enter>

The control panel reads *Enter range to copy TO: B6.* You want to copy the £ sign to cells C6 - H6 inclusive. You have learnt that the next keystrokes are .(full stop), move cursor to H6, and <Enter>. You may find the following to be easier:

Press | `.(full stop)` | `< → >` | six times | `<Enter>`

You omitted to move the cursor to C6 before anchoring the cursor with the full stop. This means that you copied cell B6 on to itself, as well as to the cells to the right. Why not, if it's easier?

6. Entering the inflows

Press | `< ↓ > < ← >` | (Cell A7)

Type | `CASH INFLOWS:` | <Enter>

You will notice that this label overflows into cell B7, but unlike your entries into cells A1 and B1, this does now matter, since you wish to enter figures into column B.

You must now widen column A to accomodate the maximum number of letters and spaces you wish to enter into it. If you refer to the table in paragraph 3 above, you will see that the longest label from the first column is:

NET CASH FLOW: A - B

There are a total of 20 letters and spaces. So you need to widen column A to 20, as follows:

Press | `/WCS20` | <Enter>

You could have used the < → > key (as you did in session 2, 4) but in this case typing *20* is quicker.

You will notice that the worksheet is now larger than can be seen at once on the screen. Columns G and H are off-screen to the right. This does not matter, but since columns B - H inclusive are wider than you need, you can, for convenience narrow columns B - H from 9 to 7 characters:

Press $\boxed{\texttt{/WGC7<Enter>}}$ (Worksheet, Global, Column-Width)

This / Worksheet, Global ({AEA} General), Column-width command sets the default column-width for every column on the worksheet which has not already been individually set beforehand by /WCS. Since you altered column A by /WCS to a width of 20, column A remains unaffected by this global setting.

[Note: {VP} has a /RCS (Range, Column-width, Set) command, which you could use as an alternative in this instance, as follows:

Move cursor to cell B7

Press $\boxed{\texttt{/RCS}}$ Move cursor to H7 Press <Enter>

Type $\boxed{\texttt{7}}$ <Enter>

This gives columns B - H only a width of 7. In {VP} /WGC sets the default column-width for all columns of the worksheet which have not been individually set beforehand by either /WCS or /RCS.]

Now you can enter the detailed inflows:

Move the cursor to cell A8

Type $\boxed{\texttt{Salary}}$ $\boxed{\texttt{<a>}}$ $\boxed{\texttt{700}}$ $\boxed{\texttt{<Enter>}}$

Next, copy the 700 in cell B8 to cells C8 - G8 inclusive, as you did for the £ sign in row 6:

Press $\boxed{\texttt{/C<Enter>.}}$ $\boxed{\texttt{<a>}}$ 5 times $\boxed{\texttt{<Enter>}}$ (Cell B8)

Now move the cursor to cell H8 (press <F5>h8<Enter>), where you require the total of the figures in cells B8 - G8 inclusive:

Press $\boxed{\texttt{@sum(b8.g8)}}$ <Enter>

The figure of 4200 should appear in cell H8, with the formula in the status line of the control panel. [If the figure 0 appears in cell H8, make sure you have not entered the values of 700 as labels!]

Note that entering the formula requires only a single fullstop, though the control panel shows two full stops.

The formula @SUM totals all figures in the range entered between the brackets. This is simpler than entering: +b8+c8+d8+e8+f8+g8 as the formula.

Press $\boxed{\texttt{<f5>b9}}$ $\boxed{\texttt{<Enter>}}$ (Cell B9)

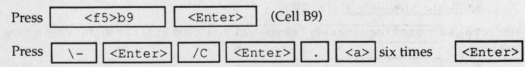

Press $\boxed{\texttt{\\-}}$ $\boxed{\texttt{<Enter>}}$ $\boxed{\texttt{/C}}$ $\boxed{\texttt{<Enter>}}$ $\boxed{\texttt{.}}$ $\boxed{\texttt{<a>}}$ six times $\boxed{\texttt{<Enter>}}$

A line a hyphens should extend from cell B9 to cell H9.

Press $\boxed{\texttt{<F5>a10<Enter>}}$ (Cell A10)

Type | Total Inflows A | | <-→> | (Cell B10)

Press | +b8 | | <Enter> | | /C | | <Enter> | | . | | <-→> | six times | <Enter> |

This enters the formula +B8 into cell B10 (thereby copying the number 700 from cell B8 into cell B10), and then copies this formula to cells C10 to H10 inclusive.

Move the cursor over cells B10 to H10, and notice the formulae displayed on the status line of the control panel as you do so.

Press | <F5>b11<Enter> | (Cell B11)

Press | \= | | <Enter> | | /C | | <Enter> | | . | | <-→> | six times | <Enter> |

This enters a row of = signs from cells B11 to H11.

7. Saving your worksheet

Before you enter the Cash Outflows, why not save the worksheet so far?

Check that you will be saving the worksheet to the correct drive and directory. If you have forgoten how to do this, refer to session 2, paragraph 13.

Press | /FS |

Type | bristol | <Enter>

and the worksheet so far is saved to a file BRISTOL.WKS or BRISTOL.WK1 (depending on the program you are using) in the drive and directory you have specified.

You should get into the habit of saving your worksheet frequently with /FS. The next time you decide to do so, say in 10 minutes time, type **/FS<Enter>R**. The 'R' is for *replace*, i.e. to replace or update the worksheet as previousy saved with the name *BRISTOL*.

[You could, if you wish, save the file separately each time you save it, e.g. with the names *BRISTOL, BRISTOL1, BRISTOL2*, and so on. The advantage of this is that if you decide that the changes you have made since you saved the worksheet for the first time as *BRISTOL* are not to your liking, you could retrieve *BRISTOL* and make new changes. You will learn how to retrieve a file in the next session.]

8. Entering the outflows

Move the cursor to cell A11

Type | CASH OUTFLOWS: | | <↓> | (Cell A12)

Type | Rates | <Enter>

Move the cursor to cell E12, and

Type [160] <Enter>

In cell H12, you want the total of cells B12..G12. To do so, you will copy the formula from cell H8, as follows:

Move the cursor to cell H8

Type [/C] <Enter>

Move the cursor to cell H12

Type [<Enter>]

Move the cursor from H8 to H12, and inspect the formula on the status line of the control panel. You will see that it reads:

@SUM(B12..G12)

Next, type in the labels for cells A13 to A19 inclusive:

Cell	Label
A13	Rent
A14	Electricity
A15	Travel
A16	Insurances
A17	Sundries
A18	Food
A19	Holiday

Next, type in the figures from the Bristol: Cash Flow Forecast sheet in paragraph 3 above, into cells B13..G19. (This is how to define a rectangular range of cells, by defining the top left and bottom right corners.) Leave the blank cells empty.

Do NOT enter the total column figures into column H, because these will be represented by formulae.

Did you take advantage of the arrow keys (when entering figures) and also the /Copy command for copying identical figures?

Now for the total formulae in cells H13..H19.

Move the cursor to cell H12

Type [/C<Enter>.] (Don't forget the full stop!)

Move the cursor to cell H19, and press <Enter>

The correct totals should now appear in cell H13..H19, and the status line of the control panel should show the appropriate formula for each cell.

Move the cursor to cell B20

Type [\-] <Enter> [/C] <Enter> [.]

Move the cursor to cell H20, and press <Enter>

This produces a line of hyphens from cell B20 to H20. (Did you remember the full stop?)

Move the cursor to cell A21

Type `Total Outflows B`   `<→>`   (Cell B21)

Type `@sum(` and no more yet!

You are now going to enter the rest of the formula by pointing.

Move the cursor up to cell B12

Type `.` (a full stop)

Move the cursor down to cell B19

The status line should now read: @SUM(B12..B19 but with no end bracket. You have to supply this:

Type `)` and then press <Enter>

Cell B21 should show 530 and the status line the formula.

Next, copy the formula from B21 to cells C21..H21:

Type `/C` <Enter> `.`

Move the cursor to cell H21, and press <Enter>

Now, draw a line of = signs from B22 to H22:

Move the cursor to cell B22

Type `\=` <Enter> `/C` <Enter> `.`

Move the cursor to H22, and press <Enter>

[Why not save the worksheet to date?]

Type `/FS<Enter>R`

9. Entering the balances

Move the cursor to cell A23

Type `NET CASH FLOW A - B` `<a>`   (Cell B23)

Type `+b10-b21` <Enter>

Type `/C` <Enter> `.`

Move the cursor to H23, and press <Enter>

Note how positive and negative values are displayed

Now enter the following labels:

Cell	Label
A24	Balances:
A25	Start of month
A26	End of month
A27	\=

Move to cell B25, and type $\boxed{250}$ <Enter>

Move to cell H25, and type $\boxed{+b25}$ <Enter>

Note: the contents of cell H25 must always be the same as the figure entered in cell B25. This is because it is not the total of line 25, but the start of the month figure at the beginning of the six month period.

Move to cell B26

Type $\boxed{+b23+b25}$ <Enter>

Move the cursor to cell C25

Type $\boxed{+b26}$ <Enter>

Next, copy cell C25 to D25..G25, as follows:

Type $\boxed{/C}$ <Enter> $\boxed{.}$

Move the cursor to G25, and press <Enter>

[Do not worry about the '0's (or blanks) in the cells; the formulae will have something to work on when you have completed line 26.]

Now, copy cell B26 to C26..H26, as follows:

Move to cell B26

Type $\boxed{/C<Enter>}$ $\boxed{.}$

Move the cursor to H26, and press <Enter>

Finally, copy the = signs in cell A27 across the page:

Move to cell A27

Type $\boxed{/C<Enter>}$ $\boxed{.}$

Move the cursor to cell H27, and press <Enter>

At last! The worksheet is complete. But before you end this session, you will do a few things to improve its appearance.

10. Aligning a range of labels

The month headings in row 5 and the £ signs in row 6 are at present all left-aligned. This is because you entered them using the default label-prefix (').

Perhaps they would look better centre-aligned, as follows:

> Move the cursor to cell B5

{123}{VP}   Press | /RLC | (Range, Label, Center)

{AEA}   Press | /RPC | (Range, Prefix, Centre)

Now you will move the cursor to cell H5, but using a new technique:

> Press | <End><→> | (Cell H5)

Note: The <End> key, when pressed before any of the arrow keys, moves the cursor in the direction of the arrow key to the cell on the boundary of any empty and filled space.

[If you are outside the area of your worksheet, you can see how large the whole spreadsheet is. Try it sometime, NOT NOW! Move the cursor outside the worksheet, press <End><↓><End><→>. Lotus 123 version 2 goes to column IV and line 8192. Press <Home> to get back to cell A1.]

> Press | <↓> | (Cell H6)

This illuminates the range B5..H6 (the top-left and bottom-right corners of the range rectangle).

> Press | <Enter> |

Do you like the revised appearance? Perhaps the labels would look even better if right-aligned:

> Move the cursor to cell B5, if not there.

{123}{VP}   Press | /RLR<End><→><↓><Enter> |

{AEA}   Press | /RPR<End><→><↓><Enter> |

11. Putting commas in figures

Finally, you will put some commas into your figures,so that, for example, 4350 appears as 4,350.

> Press | /WGF, (a comma!) 0 (number 0) | <Enter>

and there you are.

As an experiment,

Press | /WGF, (a comma!) | <Enter>

Note that this time you did not alter the default decimal position from 2, and therefore all figures appear with pence added, e.g. 700 reappears as 700.00.

In addition, some of the cells are filled with asterisks (*******).

The reason is that 4,200.00 plus a blank following is 9 characters, and you have set the column widths for B..H to 7. Therefore figures which cannot fit in appear as *******.

You could alter the column widths back to 9 using /WGC9<Enter>, but in this case, to keep all the figures horizontally visible on the screen, and also because pence are unnecessary:

Press | /WGF,0<Enter> | again.

Enough for this session.

Do not forget to SAVE your BRISTOL worksheet. You will be recovering it in the next session, and printing it out.

12. Summary

In this session you should have achieved the objectives set out at the start of this session.

In particular, you should have become acquainted with:

/WGC	Worksheet Global Column-width
/RCS	{VP} Range Column Set
@SUM	the formula to total a range of cells
/RLC	Range Label Center
/RLR	Range Label Right
/WGF,	Worksheet Global Format ,(comma) to enter commas into figures, and set the decimal place

13. Activity

13.1 BRISTOL REVISED

Three months have passed, and Mr. Bristol is revising his budget to reflect the actual figures for January, February and March.

These are as shown in the table on the following page:

CASH INFLOWS: As per budget

CASH OUTFLOWS: Actual:

	JAN	FEB	MAR
Rates	–	–	–
Rent	200	200	200
Electricity	–	–	220
Travel	50	60	60
Insurances	10	60	10
Sundries	120	150	130
Food	150	150	150
Holiday	–	–	–
Total Outflows	530	620	770

Type *Actual* in each of the cells B3, C3 and D3.

Alter the figures for January to March from budget to actual. Inspect the changes to the 'Balances: End of month' figures. What is the revised budgeted balance at the end of June? Assume his budgeted figures for the next three months are unchanged, but alter his budget for food (Mr. Bristol is somewhat overweight) for the months of April, May and June, so that he will still have a £100 balance at the end of June, even after paying for his holiday.

13.2 PERSONAL BUDGET

Draw up a personal cash flow forecast for yourself for the next year, and translate it into a worksheet, using the techniques you have acquired in the current session.

Save it, and update it throughout the year with the actual figures and revised budget figures.

14. Objective test ☐ A ☐ B ☑ C ☐ D

1. If you type: **Cash Flow** and **cASH fLOW** appears on the screen, you should delete and retype after pressing

   ☐ A <Num Lock>

   ☐ B <Caps Lock>

   ☐ C <Ins>

   ☐ D <Scroll Lock>

2. To change the widths of all columns on a worksheet which have not already been changed using /WCS (or /RCS for {VP}), the keys to press are

   ☐ A /WGC

   ☐ B /WCS

   ☐ C /RGS

   ☐ D /GCS

3. To total cells D6..D12 in cell D13, the formula to enter in cell D13 is

   ☐ A '@SUM(D6..D12)

   ☐ B @SUM[D6..D12]

   ☐ C /SUM(D6..D12)

   ☐ D @SUM(D6..D12)

4. If all the labels in cells B2..H2 are left-aligned, and column H is the extreme right-hand column with any entries, in order to change all the labels in cells B2..H2 to right-aligned, the key presses required after moving the cursor to cell B2 are [{AEA} read P for L]

   ☐ A /RLC <End><-→><Enter>

   ☐ B /RLC<Enter><End><-→><Enter>

   ☐ C /RLR <End><-→><Enter>

   ☐ D /RLR<Enter><End><-→><Enter>

5. If all the currency figures entered into your worksheet have no commas, e.g. 4,000 appears as 4000, and you want to show all the figures with commas, and with pence as well, e.g. 4,000.00, the key presses required are

   ☐ A /WGFC<Enter>

   ☐ B /WGF,<Enter>

   ☐ C /WGC,<Enter>

   ☐ D /WGCC2<Enter>

6. If after the correct key presses for question 5 above, some of the cells are full of asterisks, the reason is

   ☐ A you have made a dreadful mistake

   ☐ B the computer has gone wrong

   ☐ C it's time you went to bed

   ☐ D the columns are too narrow

7. Only one of the following formulae is incomplete. It is:

    ☐ A   +D2+E2

    ☐ B   D2*E2

    ☐ C   +D2*E2

    ☐ D   @SUM(D2..E2)

8. If you entered SUM(D2.E2) in to a cell, the cell would show:

    ☐ A   SUM(D2.E2)

    ☐ B   the total of figures in cells D2 and E2

    ☐ C   ERROR in the mode indicator box

    ☐ D   none of these

9. There are the following figures in the following cells:

Cell	Figure
C4	23
D4	34
C5	12
D5	45

    To get a total of 114 in cell B5, the formula to be entered into cell B5 is

    ☐ A   +C4+D4+C5+D5

    ☐ B   @SUM(D4..C5)

    ☐ C   @SUM(C4..D5)

    ☐ D   any of these

10. If you have saved your file with /fs several times, and then make some subsequent alterations, without saving it, if you then quit and turn off the computer,

    ☐ A   only the alterations are lost

    ☐ B   the whole file is lost

    ☐ C   only the first 'save' is saved

    ☐ D   none of these

41

SESSION 4
Printing Your Worksheet

1. Objectives

At the end of this session you will be able to:
- ❑ retrieve a worksheet
- ❑ prepare your printer
- ❑ obtain a print-out of your worksheet
- ❑ adjust the page-length for your type of paper
- ❑ print your worksheet in condensed print
- ❑ adjust the margins of your print-out
- ❑ look at all the formulae in your worksheet

2. Introduction

In this session, you will learn how to retrieve and print out the 'BRISTOL' worksheet which you created and saved in session 3.

You will also learn how to look at all the formulae of your spreadsheet rather than one at a time in the control panel.

3. Retrieving your worksheet

In session 2, you learnt how to save a worksheet in the directory of your choice. It is probably a good idea at the beginning of a session to make that directory the current directory. This could save time when you come to save and retrieve worksheets.

If you have forgotten how to use the /FD command, refer back to session 2, paragraph 13.

[Note: {123} {VP} If you regularly use one directory only,

Press | /WGDD | (Worksheet, Global, Default, Directory)

and edit the 'Directory at startup:' to your requirements.

Press | <Enter>UQ | (<Enter>, Update, Quit)

This will ensure that you have the correct directory each time you start a session after previously quitting the program.]

Make sure that the mode indicator shows READY.

Press [/FR] (File, Retrieve)

A list of files in the current directory appears in the control panel or on a drop-down menu. If BRISTOL.WKS or BRISTOL.WK1 is not shown, use the cursor (using the arrow keys) to find it. You can move the cursor off the screen or menu to see more files. Usually the cursor movement is circular, i.e. when you go beyond the end of the menu, the cursor moves back to the beginning.

{123} In addition you can press <F3>, (the List Names key) if you want to view more files at the same time.

When the cursor is over your BRISTOL file name,

Press [<Enter>] to retrieve it on to the screen.

4. Preparing your printer

Your printer should be properly connected to your computer. Make sure that it is switched on and 'On Line'. Printers vary in the facilities provided, but usually there is a light to show when it is 'On Line'. Some printers have 'Form Feed' and 'Line Feed' buttons which operate when the printer is 'Off Line', and move perforated tractor feed paper to the next perforation (Form Feed) or one line at a time (Line Feed).

Before you print your worksheet, assuming you are using continuous (perforated tractor feed paper), make sure the print head is just below the page perforation. You can do this by Form Feed or Line Feed (if the printer can do so) or by manually turning the platen knob. Some printers can be damaged if you manually turn the platen knob while the printer is turned on. Be on the safe side, and read your printer manual!

It is also good practice to tell your program that the print head is in fact at the top of a page.

Press [/PPAQ] (Print, Printer, Align, Quit)

[Note: {AEA} The keypress A is named Adjust, not Align]

The 'Quit' returns you to READY mode. Using the *Align* command should be part of your printing routine as you will see shortly.

5. Basic printing of the 'Bristol' worksheet

The following instructions assume that your printer 'default' is to print in some orthodox manner, e.g. draft at 10 cpi (characters per inch). You will learn how to change this later on. The odds are that the following instructions will produce a basic printout of your 'BRISTOL' worksheet.

(1) Make sure you have the 'BRISTOL' worksheet on the screen.

(2) Check that the mode operator is at READY, and that the cursor is in cell A1 (Press <Home> if it is not).

(3) Press [/PPR] (Print, Printer, Range)

43

The control panel displays *Enter Print range: A1*

(4) Press ⟨ `. (full-stop)` ⟩

(5) Move the cursor to cell H27. This can be done as follows:

Press ⟨ `<End><Home>` ⟩

(This moves the cursor to the bottom right hand corner of the worksheet you have created, and highlights the range A1..H27.)

(6) Press ⟨ `<Enter>` ⟩

(7) Press ⟨ `AGP` ⟩ (Align, Go, Page)

Align has been explained above in paragraph 4. *Go* instructs the printer to print the worksheet. *Page* instructs the printer to advance the paper to the top of the next sheet.

(8) Press ⟨ `Q` ⟩ (Quit)

This leaves the *Print* menu, and returns you to READY mode.

Your printout should be a replica of the worksheet on the screen, excluding the borders (column letters and row numbers) and information from the control panel.

> *Your printout should look something like Figure 4a, with column letters and row numbers added for you to refer to.*

[If the £ signs did not print, try replacing them with # signs on the worksheet (Cells B6..H6) and press /AGP again]

Before you continue, save your settings in the present worksheet:

Press ⟨ `/FS<Enter>R` ⟩

6. Adjusting the page-length

Check that the *Page* command worked. If you are using continuous stationery, the perforation should be just below the printhead, as it was before you printed the worksheet. If it is not, adjust the paper from the printer, as instructed above in paragraph 4.

Press ⟨ `/PPOP` ⟩ (Print, Printer, Options, Page-length)

The message in the control panel will read:

Enter *Lines per Page (1..100):* followed by a number, which may be the default number 66.

If you are using 8.5" by 11" paper, assuming your printer prints 6 lines per inch, then the number should be 66 lines per page, i.e. 11" times 6 lines per inch = 66 lines. If the default 66 is showing in the control panel, accept it and return to READY mode by pressing ⟨Enter⟩QQ.

Figure 4a

	A	B	C	D	E	F	G	H
1	B. BRISTOL: CASH FLOW FORECAST							
2	for the six month period January - June							
3								
4	-------							
5		JAN	FEB	MAR	APL	MAY	JUN	TOTAL
6		£	£	£	£	£	£	£
7	CASH INFLOWS							
8	Salary	700	700	700	700	700	700	4,200
9								
10	Total Inflows A	700	700	700	700	700	700	4,200
11	CASH OUTFLOWS:							
12	Rates				160			160
13	Rent	200	200	200	200	200	200	1,200
14	Electricity			180			180	360
15	Travel	50	50	50	50	50	50	300
16	Insurances	10	40	10	130	10	10	210
17	Sundries	120	120	120	120	120	120	720
18	Food	150	150	150	150	150	150	900
19	Holiday						500	500
20								
21	Total Outflows B	530	560	710	810	530	1,210	4,350
22								
23	NET CASH FLOW: A - B	170	140	(10)	(110)	170	(510)	(150)
24	Balances:							
25	Start of month	250	420	560	550	440	610	250
26	End of month	420	560	550	440	610	100	100
27								

If, however you are using A4 continuous paper, which is 8.25" by 11.67", then the number should be changed (typed over) to 70, which is 11.67" times 6 lines per inch = 70 lines, before pressing <Enter>QQ.

If you have any other size paper, measure it and use the above principles to calculate the correct number of lines.

This corrects the page length for the current worksheet.

[Note: {123} {VP} If you want to adjust the page-length for all future sessions (i.e. alter the global default setting):

Press `/WGDPP` (Worksheet, Global, Default, Printer, Page-Length)

Type in the page-length you require, then:

Press `<Enter>QUQ` (Quit, Update, Quit) to return to READY.]

45

7. Printing in condensed print

In paragraph 5, you printed the BRISTOL worksheet at your printer's default, probably at 10 cpi (characters per inch).

You can calculate how many characters wide the worksheet is, as follows:

Column A	20
Columns B – H, 7 columns x 7 characters =	49
Total	69

Normal screens are able to display 72 or 76 characters (depending on the program). Many printers are able to print 80 characters on 8.5" wide or A4 paper. A normal default for a spreadsheet program is 72 characters, and later you will learn how to change this.

However, assuming that 72 is a normal limit, this means that the BRISTOL worksheet, at 69 characters, just managed to print out without some right-hand columns being printed below the other columns.

There are several solutions to printing out wide worksheets which will not fit normal 8.5" or A4 paper at 10 cpi. One is to alter the cpi from 10 cpi to, say, 17 cpi.

This is called compressed (or small) print. If your printer is a dot-matrix printer (and not a daisy-wheel) printer you should be able to change to this.

With the BRISTOL worksheet retrieved, and in READY mode,

Press ` /PPOS ` (Print, Printer, Options, Set-up)

You should see the prompt in the control panel:

Enter Setup String:

This where you enter some codes to tell your printer to print in compressed print. The codes vary from printer to printer.

If your printer is an Epson (or Epson-compatible) the code to try is \027\015 or \015. [For {AEA} press \<F1>, move the cursor to CND-ON and press <Enter>. This enters the code \015 for you!]

If this code does not work, consult your printer manual for the decimal code for compressed print. Note that it must be the decimal code. If the code is given in another format, e.g. ESC+SI or 1B,0F (Hex. code) for 027,015 (decimal), you will have to look up a conversion table to convert it to decimal format. Note also that the decimal three-digit codes must be preceded by a back-slash.

Some printers can also be set to print in condensed print from the printer's operator panel. (The printer manual should explain how to do this.) If this is possible, then it is not necessary to enter a printer set-up string from the spreadsheet program.

{123} {VP} If you wish to clear a set-up string which you already entered to the global default (usually blank), **press /PPCFQ** (Print, Printer, Clear, Format, Quit).

{AEA} To clear a set-up string, press /PPOS<Esc>

When you have entered the set-up string,

Press │ <Enter>QQ │ to return to READY mode.

If you now want to print out in compressed print, follow the procedure in paragraph 5 above. If you saved the range settings, then the keystrokes are:

Press │ /PPAGP │ (Print, Printer, Align, Go, Page)

With any luck, you should obtain a print-out in compressed print, and the paper (if continuous) should be at the top of the next sheet.

8. Adjusting the margins

Your print-out in compressed print will be at the top left-hand corner of your paper.

It is possible to move your print-out to a more central position by altering the margin settings.

{123} {VP} If you wish to see the current default settings,

Press │ /WGDS │ (Worksheet, Global, Default, Status)

You will see such items as your current defaults for page-length and printer set-up strings.

{AEA} You will see the defaults later, when you press /PPOM.

Margins are what we are interested in at present.

The defaults are probably (unless somebody has changed them):

Left: 4   Right: 76   Top: 2   Bottom: 2

{AEA} The defaults are Left: 0 Right: 80

The top and bottom margins are the distance in lines of print from the top and bottom edges of the paper default, e.g. 66 lines from top to bottom. If you changed the default in paragraph 6 above to 70 (for A4 paper) the default shows as 70 lines.

How many lines of your worksheet can be printed out on one page can be calculated as follows:

Assume that the page-length is set for 66 lines, and top and bottom margins at 2 lines each. You might expect that 66 less 2 less 2 = 62 lines of worksheet can be printed. However, the programs (unless you change the settings) allow in addition for headers and footers, i.e. items which can be typed in at the top and bottom of each page.

{123}{VP} One line of header or footer can be typed in, and the programs allow 2 extra lines of space between these single lines and the text. Thus 6 extra lines (3 for headers and 3 for footers) have to be deducted, i.e. 62 less 6 – 56 lines.

{AEA} One line of header or footer can be typed in, and the program allows 1 extra line of space between these single lines and the text. One line at the top and bottom of the page is reserved for a perf-skip feature. Thus 6 extra lines have to be deducted, i.e. 62 less 6 = 56 lines.

The following table should make this clear:

Program	{123}	{VP}	{AEA}	
Paper type	11"	A4	11"	A4
Perf-skip			1	1
Top margin	2	2	2	2
Header space	3	3	2	2
Body of text	56	60	56	60
Footer space	3	3	2	2
Bottom margin	2	2	2	2
Perf-skip			1	1
	66	70	66	70

[Note: headers and footers will be covered in a later session]

The left and right margin figures are the distance in *characters* from the *left-hand side of the paper*. This is a frequent cause of misunderstanding. [Some students assume that the right margin figure is measured from the right-hand side of the paper, and set the margin figure accordingly, say at 6 characters. This would result in a very narrow print-out of 2 (6 minus 4) characters!]

Now for some calculations. Your *BRISTOL* worksheet is 69 characters wide. With compressed print at 17 cpi, you should be able to get, say, 8 inches times 17 cpi = 136 characters on your A4 or 8.5" x 11" paper. In order to centre the printout, you could have a margin each side of 136 minus 69 = 67 divided by two = (say) 33 characters. So you could set the left margin at 33, and the right margin at 33 plus 69 = 102 (not forgetting that the measurement is from the left-hand edge of the paper.

The *BRISTOL* worksheet is 27 rows deep. Assume you have 56 lines available for printing on your paper (see above for {123}{VP} 11" paper). This means you have 56 - 27 = 29 lines spare. In order to centre the worksheet approximately you could increase the top margin of 2 lines by half the 29 spare lines, say 14, and alter the top margin to 16 lines.

Now to try it out, remembering that you are adjusting the margins for the current worksheet only:

Press | /PPOM | (Print, Printer, Options, Margins)

The control panel reads: *Left*   *Right*   *Top*   *Bottom*

Press | L33<Enter>

[You are returned to the Margins menu each time.]

Press | MR102<Enter>

48

Press   `MT16<Enter>`

Press   `MB2<Enter>`   or   `MB<Enter>`   if 2 is displayed.

Assuming you have not changed your printer set-up string, your range or page-length, to print out:

Press   `Q`   (Quit returns you to the Printer sub-menu)

Press   `AGPQ`   (Align, Go, Page, Quit)

Your printout should look something like Figure 4b, with column letters and row numbers added for you to refer to.

Figure 4b

	A	B	C	D	E	F	G	H
1	B. BRISTOL: CASH FLOW FORECAST							
2	for the six month period January - June							
3								
4	--							
5		JAN	FEB	MAR	APL	MAY	JUN	TOTAL
6		£	£	£	£	£	£	£
7	CASH INFLOWS							
8	Salary	700	700	700	700	700	700	4,200
9				--				
10	Total Inflows A	700	700	700	700	700	700	4,200
11	CASH OUTFLOWS:	===						
12	Rates				160			160
13	Rent	200	200	200	200	200	200	1,200
14	Electricity			180			180	360
15	Travel	50	50	50	50	50	50	300
16	Insurances	10	40	10	130	10	10	210
17	Sundries	120	120	120	120	120	120	720
18	Food	150	150	150	150	150	150	900
19	Holiday						500	500
20			--					
21	Total Outflows B	530	560	710	810	530	1,210	4,350
22		===						
23	NET CASH FLOW: A	170	140	(10)	(110)	170	(510)	(150)
24	Balances:							
25	Start of month	250	420	560	550	440	610	250
26	End of month	420	560	550	440	610	100	100
27		===						

9. Looking at the formulae

You can, of course, inspect the formula for a particular cell by positioning the cursor on it, and reading the formula from the status line of the control panel.

Sometimes, however, it is useful to be able to look at all the formulae.

Before you do so, save your BRISTOL worksheet and the margin changes you have made with /FS<Enter>R.

Press [/WGFT] (Worksheet, Global, Format, Text)

Now you can see the formulae, but some of them are too wide to fit in the columns.

You must widen columns B..H. How wide? The longest formula is, for example, in cell B21: @SUM(B12..B19), i.e 15 characters (including a space after the final bracket).

Press [/WGC] (Worksheet, Global, Column-Width)

Press [15<Enter>] (or move <→> until width is 15 <Enter>)

You should now be able to see all the formulae, though the whole worksheet is no longer visible on the screen. You will have to move the cursor to see columns which are off-screen.

Now save this file under the name BRISTOLF (the F is for formulae).

Press [/FS]   Type [BRISTOLF]   Press [<Enter>]

Figure 4c is a printout of this file.

Figure 4c

B. BRISTOL: CASH FLOW FORECAST
for the six month period January - June

```
                     JAN           FEB           MAR           APL           MAY           JUN           TOTAL
                     £             £             £             £             £             £             £
CASH INFLOWS
Salary               700           700           700           700           700           700           @SUM(B8..G8)
                    ------------------------------------------------------------------------------------------------
Total Inflows A +B8                +C8           +D8           +E8           +F8           +G8           +H8
CASH OUTFLOWS:       =======================================================================================================
Rates                                                          160                                       @SUM(B12..G12)
Rent                 200           200           200           200           200           200           @SUM(B13..G13)
Electricity                                                    180                                       @SUM(B14..G14)
Travel               50            50            50            50            50            50            @SUM(B15..G15)
Insurances           10            40            10            130           10            10            @SUM(B16..G16)
Sundries             120           120           120           120           120           120           @SUM(B17..G17)
Food                 150           150           150           150           150           150           @SUM(B18..G18)
Holiday                                                                                    500           @SUM(B19..G19)
                    ------------------------------------------------------------------------------------------------
Total Outflows B@SUM(B12..B19) @SUM(C12..C19) @SUM(D12..D19) @SUM(E12..E19) @SUM(F12..F19) @SUM(G12..G19) @SUM(H12..H19)
                    =======================================================================================================
NET CASH FLOW: ,+B10-B21          +C10-C21      +D10-D21      +E10-E21      +F10-F21      +G10-G21      +H10-H21
Balances:
Start of month 250                +B26          +C26          +D26          +E26          +F26          +B25
End of month   +B23+B25           +C23+C25      +D23+D25      +E23+E25      +F23+F25      +G23+G25      +H23+H25
                    =======================================================================================================
```

In order to see the worksheet as it was, without the formulae in the cells,

Press [/WGFG] (Worksheet, Global, Format, General)

The worksheet has now been saved as BRISTOL (with revised margin settings) and BRISTOLF (with formulae showing and wider columns) and there is no need to save it again. In fact, if you saved it now, it would have column-widths saved which are wider than necessary.

You can end this session in the normal way. If you have forgotten how, refer back to session 1, paragraph 12.

10. Summary

In this session you should have achieved the objectives set out at the start of this session.

In particular, you should have become acquainted with:

/WGDD	Worksheet, Global, Default, Directory *
/FR	File, Retrieve
/PPAQ	Print, Printer, Align, Quit
/PPR	Print, Printer, Range
/PPAGP	Print, Printer, Align, Go, Page
/PPOP	Print, Printer, Options, Page-length
/WGDPP	Worksheet, Global, Default, Printer, Page-length
/PPOS	Print, Printer, Options, Set-up
/WGDS	Worksheet, Global, Default, Status *
/PPOM	Print, Printer, Options, Margins
/WGFT	Worksheet, Global, Format, Text
/WGFG	Worksheet, Global, Format, General

Note * = not [AEA]

11. Activity

Print out the BRISTOLF worksheet, showing all the formulae.

Hints: You will have to alter the margins. The principles for the calculations were demonstrated in paragraph 8 above. Check that the correct range is specified and that the printer set-up string is correct for condensed print.

12. Objective test ☐ A ☐ B ☑ C ☐ D

1. In order to retrieve a worksheet file which you have already saved, the keystrokes required to retrieve it from the READY mode are

    ☐ A /WR

    ☐ B \WR

    ☐ C /FR

    ☐ D \FR

2. In order to tell your program that your printer is at the top of a new page, and to return to READY mode, the keypresses, from READY mode, are

    ☐ A /PPA

    ☐ B /PPAQ

    ☐ C /PAQ

    ☐ D /SPQR

3. You wish to define the range A1..H27 for printing where H27 is the bottom right-hand corner of your worksheet. From READY mode the keypresses are

    ☐ A /PPR.<End><Home><Enter>

    ☐ B /PRP.<Home><End><Enter>

    ☐ C /PPR<Enter>.<Home><End><Enter>

    ☐ D /PRP<Enter>.<Home><End><Enter>

4. In order to adjust the page length from the present default of 66 lines to 70 lines (for A4 paper), the keypresses from READY mode are

    ☐ A /PPP70<Enter>

    ☐ B /PPOP<Enter>70<Enter>

    ☐ C /POPPY70<Enter>

    ☐ D /PPOP70<Enter>

5. In order to enter a set-up string to instruct your printer to use condensed print, the keypresses from READY mode are

    ☐ A /PPS

    ☐ B /POPS

    ☐ C /PPOS

    ☐ D /PPROS

6. The set-up string for an Epson (or compatible) printer for condensed print is

   ☐ A /027/015

   ☐ B \027\015

   ☐ C \015\027

   ☐ D /015/027

7. You have defined the range settings, adjusted the page-length and entered any required set-up string ready for printing. In order to print your file, the keypresses from READY mode are

   ☐ A /PPAGP

   ☐ B /AGP

   ☐ C /PPGAP

   ☐ D /PPAP

8. You have pressed /PPOML6<Enter> to give you a margin of 6 characters from the left-hand side of the page. You now wish to set the right-hand margin to 6 characters from the right-hand side of the page which you calculate is 82 characters from the left-hand side of the page. The keypresses are

   ☐ A MR76<Enter>

   ☐ B R76<Enter>

   ☐ C MR6<Enter>

   ☐ D R6<Enter>

9. In order to see all the formulae, rather than the values resulting from the formulae, of your worksheet, the keypresses from READY mode are

   ☐ A /WFGT

   ☐ B /WGFT

   ☐ C /WGFG

   ☐ D /WFTG

10. Following the correct keypresses in question 9 above, to return to normal values, rather than formulae, visible in the cells, the keypresses from READY mode are

   ☐ A /WFGT

   ☐ B /WGGF

   ☐ C /WGFG

   ☐ D /WFTG

SESSION 5
Pontefract Financial Budgets

1. Objectives

At the end of this session you will be able to:

- ❑ create a worksheet into which you can enter data and from which a cash flow forecast, trading and profit & loss account, and balance sheet are automatically produced and updated
- ❑ understand what is meant by a data-block
- ❑ learn more about formulae, particularly + - * /
- ❑ save and print various versions of the same worksheet
- ❑ understand the logical function @IF
- ❑ protect labels and formulae from inadvertant alteration

2. Introduction

In this session, you will create a worksheet which is the solution to a budgeting problem.

The problem is adapted from an example in AFBIS (chapter entitled *The Relationship between Financial Statements*) and is set out in full in paragraph 3 below.

The solution to this problem is set out in figures 5a and 5b, which are a printout of the worksheet which you will create.

In order to create this worksheet, you will not be given individual keypresses as you were in the previous sessions. Instead, you are referred to figures 5c and 5d, which show the whole worksheet with column letters, row numbers, labels, values and formulae.

Most of the format of this worksheet will be familiar to you from what you have learnt in the previous sessions. There are some new aspects, however, and these are explained in paragraphs 4 and following.

You are advised to make your worksheet an exact replica of figures 5c and 5d, so that when you print it out, it should look like figures 5a and 5b.

This is not so formidable a task as you might think. You will be given advice about column-widths and margin settings etc., though should feel free to experiment for yourself.

If you find this session too much for one sitting, don't forget to save your work before leaving the program! It is good practice to save your work every 10 minutes or so in any case.

It is suggested that you save the worksheet with the filename PONTEF01. Then you can save subsequent versions as PONTEFxx, where xx represents various version references.

The problem and comments on its solution follow in paragraphs 3 and 4. It is not essential that you understand these in order to create the worksheet, though it is obviously better if you do!

3. Pontefract: The problem

Peter Pontefract has inherited £30,000, and plans to commence a confectionery business trading as PONTEFRACT on 1st April, 19x1.

His plans include the following:

(1) Equipment costing £16,000 will be bought and paid for on 1st April. Further equipment will be bought and paid for on 1st July, costing £8,000. Peter estimates that this equipment will last 10 years with no scrap value, and he will charge depreciation in his accounts from the date of purchase on a straight-line basis.

(2) Wages will be £2,000 per month for the first 3 months, and £3,000 per month thereafter.

(3) Selling and administration costs are expected to be £1,200 per month for the first 3 months, rising to £1,400 per month thereafter, payable in the month when the costs are incurred.

(4) Premises will be rented at £7,200 per annum, payable quarterly in advance starting on 1st April, 19x1.

(5) Selling price of goods is calculated at purchase price plus 50%.

(6) Terms of trade are for customers to pay in the month following receipt of goods, and Peter has arranged with his suppliers for payment to be made two months after the month of purchase.

Peter's planned sales and purchases are:

	Sales (£000s)	Purchases (£000s)
April	12	30
May	16	24
June	20	20
July	24	20
August	24	20
September	24	20
Totals	120	134

Required:

Prepare for PONTEFRACT the following BUDGETED documents:

(a) Cash Flow Forecast for the first 6 months of trading, showing the expected bank balances at the end of each month.

(b) Trading and Profit & Loss Account for the 6 months to 30.9.19x1.

(c) Balance Sheet as at 30.9.19x1.

4. Pontefract: The solution

The solution to this problem is set out in figures 5a and 5b.

The workings are as follows:

(1)

	Sales (£000s)		Purchases (£000s)	
	Invoiced	Cash	Invoiced	Paid
April	12		30	
May	16	12	24	
June	20	16	20	30
July	24	20	20	24
August	24	24	20	20
September	24	24	20	20
Totals	120	96	134	94
Debtors		24	Creditors	40
		120		134

(2) Depreciation of equipment:

£16,000 x 10% p.a. = £1,600 p.a.: 6 months = £800
£8,000 x 10% p.a. = £800 p.a.: 3 months = £200
£1,000

(3) Stock: See Trading Account (Figure 5b, Table C):

Sales are £120,000 (data) which is 50% added on to cost of sales - see note (5) of problem (para. 3 above).

Cost of sales is therefore two-thirds of sales value, i.e. £80,000.

Stock is therefore the difference between purchases of £134,000 (data) and cost of sales of £80,000.

5. Notes on the design of the worksheet

Please refer to figures 5a, 5b, 5c and 5d.

Figure 5a

	A	B	C	D	E	F	G	H
1	PONTEFRACT							
2	===							
3	TABLE A: DATA							
4	Month:	April	May	June	July	August	Sept	Total
5		£	£	£	£	£	£	£
6	Capital	30,000						
7	Equipment	16,000			8,000			24,000
8	Nages	2,000	2,000	2,000	3,000	3,000	3,000	15,000
9	Selling & Admin	1,200	1,200	1,200	1,400	1,400	1,400	7,800
10	Rent of Premises	1,800			1,800			3,600
11	Sales	12,000	16,000	20,000	24,000	24,000	24,000	120,000
12	Purchases	30,000	24,000	20,000	20,000	20,000	20,000	134,000
13	Cash at start	0						
14	===							
15	TABLE B: CASH FLOW FORECAST for the first six months of trading							
16								
17	Month:	April	May	June	July	August	Sept	Total
18		£	£	£	£	£	£	£
19	RECEIPTS:							
20	Capital	30,000						30,000
21	Sales		12,000	16,000	20,000	24,000	24,000	96,000
22								--------
23	Total A	30,000	12,000	16,000	20,000	24,000	24,000	126,000
24								========
25	PAYMENTS							
26	Purchases			30,000	24,000	20,000	20,000	94,000
27	Wages	2,000	2,000	2,000	3,000	3,000	3,000	15,000
28	Selling & Admin	1,200	1,200	1,200	1,400	1,400	1,400	7,800
29	Rent	1,800	0	0	1,800	0	0	3,600
30	Equipment	16,000	0	0	8,000	0	0	24,000
31								--------
32	Total B	21,000	3,2CO	33,200	38,200	24,400	24,400	144,400
33								========
34	NET CASH FLOW A-B	9,000	8,800	(17,200)	(18,200)	(400)	(400)	(18,400)
35								--------
36	Balances:							
37	Start of month	0	9,000	17,800	600	(17,600)	(18,000)	0
38	End of month	9,000	17,800	600	(17,600)	(18,000)	(18,400)	(18,400)
39	===							

Figure 5b

	A	B	C	D	E	F	G	H
40	TABLE C: BUDGETED TRADING AND PROFIT & LOSS ACCOUNT for the period							
41	of six months ending 30th September, 19x1							
42								
43					£		£	£
44	Sales							120,000
45	less Cost of Sales:							
46	Purchases						134,000	
47	less Closing Stock						54,000	
48							-------	
49								80,000
50								-------
51	Gross Profit							40,000
52	less Expenses:							
53	Wages						15,000	
54	Selling & Admin						1,800	
55	Rent						3,600	
56	Depreciation:							
57	Original Equipment				800			
58	Later Equipment				200			
59					-------		1,000	
60							-------	27,400
61								-------
62	Net Profit							12,600
63								=======
64								
65	TABLE D: BUDGETED BALANCE SHEET as at 30th September, 19x1							
66					£		£	£
67	FIXED ASSETS			Cost			Acc.Dep'n	NBV
68	Equipment			24,000			1,000	23,000
69				=======			=======	
70	CURRENT ASSETS							
71	Stock			54,000				
72	Debtors			24,000				
73				-------			78,000	
74	CURRENT LIABILITIES							
75	Creditors			40,000				
76	Overdraft			18,400				
77				-------			58,400	
78	Net Current Assets						-------	19,600
79								-------
80	Capital Employed							42,600
81								=======
82	Represented by:							
83	Capital						30,000	
84	Profit for 6 months						12,600	
85							-------	42,600
86								=======
87	==							

58

Figure 5c

	A	B	C	D	E	F	G	H
1	PONTEFRACT							
2	==
3	TABLE A: DATA							
4	Month:		April		May		June		July		August		Sept		Total
5			£		£		£		£		£		£		£
6	Capital	30,000						
7	Equipment	16,000			8,000			@SUM(B7..G7)
8	Nages	2,000	2,000	2,000	3,000	3,000	3,000	@SUM(B8..G8)
9	Selling & Adm:	1,200	1,200	1,200	1,400	1,400	1,400	@SUM(B9..G9)
10	Rent of Premi:	1,800			1,800			@SUM(B10..G10)
11	Sales	12,000	16,000	20,000	24,000	24,000	24,000	@SUM(B11..G11)
12	Purchases	30,000	24,000	20,000	20,000	20,000	20,000	@SUM(B12..G12)
13	Cash at start	0						@SUM(B13..G13)
14	==
15	TABLE B: CASH FLOW FORECAST for the first six months of trading							
16								
17	Month:		April		May		June		July		August		Sept		Total
18			£		£		£		£		£		£		£
19	RECEIPTS:							
20	Capital	+B6						@SUM(B20..G20)
21	Sales		+B11	+C11	+D11	+E11	+F11	@SUM(B21..G21)
22			---
23	Total A	+B20	+C21	+D21	+E21	+F21	+G21	@SUM(B23..G23)
24			==
25	PAYMENTS							
26	Purchases		+B12	+C12	+D12	+E12	+G12	@SUM(B26..G26)
27	Wages	+B8	+C8	+D8	+E8	+F8	+G8	@SUM(B27..G27)
28	Selling & Adm:	+B9	+C9	+D9	+E9	+F9	+G9	@SUM(B28..G28)
29	Rent	+B10	+C10	+D10	+E10	+F10	+G10	@SUM(B29..G29)
30	Equipment	+B7	+C7	+D7	+E7	+F7	+G7	@SUM(B30..G30)
31			---
32	Total B	@SUM(B26..E	@SUM(C26..C30)	@SUM(D26..D30)	@SUM(E26..E30)	@SUM(F26..F30)	@SUM(G26..G30)	@SUM(B32..G32
33			==
34	NET CASH FLOW	+B23-B32	+C23-C32	+D23-D32	+E23-E32	+F23-F32	+G23-G32	+H23-H32
35			---
36	Balances:							
37	Start of month	+B13	+B38	+C38	+D38	+E38	+F38	+B37
38	End of month	+B34+B37	+C34+C37	+D34+D37	+E34+E37	+F34+F37	+G34+G37	+H34+H37
39	==

Figure 5d

	A	B	C	D	E	F	G	H
40	TABLE C: BUDGETED TRADING AND PROFIT & LOSS ACCOUNT for the period							
41	of six months ending 30th September, 19x1							
42								
43						£		£	£
44	Sales							+H11
45	less Cost of Sales:							
46	Purchases					+H12		
47	less Closing Stock					+F46-H49		
48						-------------		
49								+H11*2/3
50								-------------
51	Gross Profit							+H44-H49
52	less Expenses:							
53	Wages					+H8		
54	Selling & Admin					+H9		
55	Rent					+H10		
56	Depreciation:							
57	Original Equipment				+B7/10*6/12			
58	Later Equipment				+E7/10*3/12			
59					-------------	+E57+E58		
60						-------------		@SUM(F53..F59)
61								-------------
62	Net Profit							+H51-H60
63								=============
64	==							
65	TABLE D: BUDGETED BALANCE SHEET as at 30th September, 19x1							
66						£		£	£
67	FIXED ASSETS			Cost		Acc.Dep'n		NBV
68	Equipment			+H7		+F59		+D68-F68
69				=============		=============		
70	CURRENT ASSETS							
71	Stock			+F47				
72	Debtors			+H11-H21				
73				-------------		+D71+D72		
74	CURRENT LIABILITIES							
75	Creditors			+H12-H26				
76	Overdraft			-H38				
77				-------------		+D75+D76		
78	Net Current Assets					-------------		+F73-F77
79								-------------
80	Capital Employed							+H68+H78
81								=============
82	Represented by:							
83	Capital					+B6		
84	Profit for 6 months					+H62		
85						-------------		+F83+F84
86								=============
87	==							

TABLE A: DATA

This is a data-block into which the data of the problem can be entered. You will see from figure 5c that it consists mainly of labels and values. The only column which contains formulae is column H, which adds columns B..G.

[At the end of this session, you will protect (so that it cannot be inadvertently altered) all of this table except for the range B6..G13 in which the values of the data are entered.]

TABLES B, C and D

You will see from figures 5c and 5d that these tables contain only labels, and formulae which refer to cells in table A as well as cells within tables B, C and D.

[At the end of this session, you will protect all of these three tables. In other words, only the values in in the range of cells B6..G13 in table A can be altered.]

This means that, when you have created the whole worksheet, if you alter any of the data values in cells B6..G13 in table A, then the figures in the cash flow forecast, budgeted trading and profit & loss account and budgeted balance sheet will alter automatically.

6. Notes on creating the worksheet

Column A can be set at 17 characters wide.

Columns B..H can be set at 8 characters wide.

Cell H49: +H11*2/3

This formula takes cell H11 (total sales) and multiplies it by two-thirds. This gives the cost of sales figure. See paragraph 4 (3) for an explanation.

Cell F47: +F46-H49

This formula takes the contents of cell F46 (total purchases from cell H12) and deducts the contents of cell H49 (the cost of sales). This gives the closing stock figure. See paragraph 4 (3) for an explanation.

Cells E57 and E58:

These cells calculate depreciation on the equipment purchased during the six months.

For example, in cell E57 is the formula +B7/10*6/12.

This means:

+B7	£16,000 from cell B7
/10	divided by 10, because depreciation is for 10 years, straight-line method, and
*6/12	multiplied by 6 and divided by 12, i.e. 6 months of a full year's depreciation.

Similarly, the formula in cell E58, +E7/10*3/12 calculates the depreciation on the equipment to be bought in July for £8,000 for the 3 months of July to September.

Cell D76 -H38

This is the overdraft figure at the end of the six months from cell H38 in the cash flow forecast.

Since you need a positive figure under Current liabilities in the Balance Sheet, and the overdraft figure in cell H38 is negative (overdrawn), you use the minus and not the plus sign.

7. Saving and printing the worksheet

It is to be hoped that you have been saving your worksheet frequently as you created it, perhaps with the file-name PONTEF01, as suggested in paragraph 2 above.

You could now try printing it out in condensed print, using the skills acquired in session 4.

You should print out two ranges separately:

A1..H39 and A40..H87

Plan your margins carefully.

You may like to experiment as follows:

When you have successfully printed out the first range A1..H39, and are satisfied with the results, save the file as PONTEF5A. Then if ever you want to print it out again with the same settings, you can do so with no more effort.

Now retrieve PONTEF01, and print out the second range A40..H87. Again, if you are happy with the settings, save the worksheet as PONTEF5B.

If you are feeling particularly energetic, you could use /WGFT to see all the formulae. Then you could try printing out the two ranges separately, after adjusting the columns appropriately. Plan your margins very carefully! Again, these settings could be saved as PONTEF5C and PONTEF5D respectively.

8. The logical function @IF

If you want to create a balance sheet to cope with a positive (credit) balance figure at the bank, you will have to create a cell under Current Assets, e.g. at cell D73 with the reference +H38. Cell A73 could have the label ' Cash at Bank, cell F73 could have the formula +D71+D72+D73 or @SUM(D71..D73), and cell D74 could have a row of hyphens.

The problem then is that we would have the same figure from cell H38 entered twice on the balance sheet, i.e. under Current Assets in cell D73, and under Current Liabilities in cell D76.

The problem can be solved by using the logical function @IF, as follows:

Cash at Bank:　Cell D73:　　　　@IF(H38>0,H38,0)

Overdraft:　　　Cell D76　　　　　@IF(H38<0,-H38,0)

The first formula instructs the program:

If the contents of cell H38 are greater than 0 (zero), then enter the contents of cell H38 into this current cell (D73); otherwise enter 0 (zero). For the present data, since cell H38 contains (£18,400) or -£18,400, i.e. a sum less than zero, then cell D73 will read 0.

The second formula instructs the program:

If the contents of cell H38 are less than 0 (zero), then enter the (negative) contents of cell H38 into this current cell (D76) as a positive amount. For the present data, since cell H38 contains (£18,400) or -£18,400, i.e. a sum less than zero, then cell D76 will read £18,400.

> Enter these formulae into cells D73 and D76.
>
> Enter 'Cash at bank' in cell A73.
>
> Enter a line of hyphens in cell D74 (Press \-Enter>)
>
> Alter (using edit <F2>) cell F73 from the formula +D71+D72 to the formula +D71+D72+D73
>
> Alter (using edit <F2>) cell F83 from the formula +B6 to the formula +B6+B13

If you have altered PONTEF01 to incorporate these changes, why not save this revised version as PONTEF02?

Now you can try changing the data in table A, and see the effect on tables B, C and D. For example, enter cash at start (cell B13) as £20,000. You will note that cell H38 changes to £1,600 (positive), D73 to £1,600 and D76 to 0 (zero).

The balance sheet still balances, because the formula for capital in cell F83 is now +B6+B13, i.e the initial capital of £30,000 (cell B6) plus any extra cash which you inject into the business by entering it into cell B13.

[Note that in this model, if you alter sales, then the closing stock will be adjusted, not purchases. Cell H49 maintains a constant relationship between sales and cost of sales.]

9. Protecting the cells

The only cells which you wish to change are in the range B6..G13. The remaining cells can be protected from inadvertant alteration by the following:

> Retrieve worksheet PONTEF01.

{123}{VP}　　Press /WGPE (Worksheet, Global, Protection, Enable)

> This protects all the cells of the worksheet.

Move the cursor to cell B6

Press | /RU | (Range, Unprotect)

Move the cursor to cell G13, and press <Enter>

{AEA}   Move the cursor to cell B6

Press | /RLN | (Range, Lock, No)

Move the cursor to cell G13, and press <Enter>

Press | /WGPE | (Worksheet, General, Protect, Enable)

This results in cells B6..G13 being unprotected, and it is now possible to change the values in those cells, but no others.

If you do want to alter a label or formula in the protected cells, you can press /WGPD (Worksheet, Global, Protect, Disable), and then, when you have made any changes, you can re-protect with /WGPE.

You can, if you wish, get some additional practice by protecting the labels and formulae on the other versions of the Pontefract worksheet which you have saved.

10. Summary

In this session you should have achieved the objectives set out at the start of this session.

In particular, you should have become acquainted with:

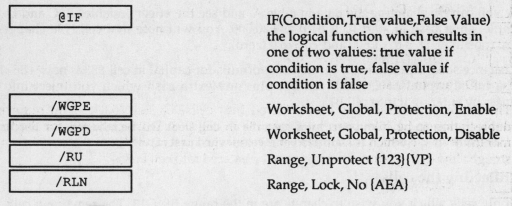

@IF	IF(Condition,True value,False Value) the logical function which results in one of two values: true value if condition is true, false value if condition is false
/WGPE	Worksheet, Global, Protection, Enable
/WGPD	Worksheet, Global, Protection, Disable
/RU	Range, Unprotect {123}{VP}
/RLN	Range, Lock, No {AEA}

17. Activity

Prepare some budgeted data for an enterprise of your choice, similar to that for Pontefract as set out in paragraph 3 above.

Try to make the values realistic in the sense that you want the business to have a satisfactory cash flow, profit and loss account, and balance sheet at the end of the six month period.

Retrieve your worksheet which you filed with the name PONTEF02, i.e the one with the facility to record either a bank balance or overdraft in the balance sheet. (See paragraph 8 above.)

Make sure that all the labels and formulae are protected. (See paragraph 9 above.)

Erase the range B6..G13, as follows:

> Move the cursor to cell B6

Press | /RE |

> Move the cursor to cell G13

Press | <Enter> |

Enter your own data, and then examine and comment on the results shown in tables B, C and D.

[Note: do not enter figures in cells C13..G13, since these will result in an incorrect capital figure in cell F83. It would, of course, be possible to adjust the design of the worksheet to accommodate this, but this is beyond the scope of this session.]

12. Objective test ☐ A ☐ B ☑ C ☐ D

1. The formula to add the values in cells D14..D17 is

    ☐ A @SUM(D14..D17)

    ☐ B @SUM(D17..D14)

    ☐ C +D14+D15+D16+D17

    ☐ D any of these

2. The value of an asset has been entered into cell D68 as £20,000. You require its depreciation to be calculated by a formula in cell F68. Depreciation is for the first 9 months of its life which is estimated at 5 years with no scrap value at the end. Assuming straight-line depreciaton, the formula to be entered into cell F68 is

    ☐ A £20,000/5x9/12

    ☐ B +D68/60x9

    ☐ C +D68/5*9/12

    ☐ D +D68+5x9+12

3. You have retrieved a file named WEARY. You have improved it, and want to save it in its new form while, at the same time preserving the file in its original form. To do so you press

    ☐ A /FS<Enter>WEARY01<Enter>R

    ☐ B /FSWEARY01<Enter>

    ☐ C /FSR<Enter>R<Enter>

    ☐ D none of these

4. You wish to protect all the cells of your current worksheet. The keypresses are

    ☐ A /RGPE

    ☐ B /RPE<Enter>

    ☐ C /WGPE<Enter>

    ☐ D /WGPE

5. You have correctly protected all the cells of your current worksheet. You wish to unprotect a range within the worksheet. The initial keypresses, before pointing the required range, are

    ☐ A /RU or /RLN {AEA}

    ☐ B /UR or /LNR {AEA}

    ☐ C /RRU or /RRLN {AEA}

    ☐ D /URU or /RNLI {AEA}

6. The @IF is a

    ☐ A statistical function

    ☐ B logical function

    ☐ C financial function

    ☐ D none of these

7. The following describes the @IF function:

    ☐ A (True value,False value,Condition)

    ☐ B (Condition,False value,True value)

    ☐ C (Condition,True value,False value)

    ☐ D none of these

66

8. The following is a correct entry for an @IF function:

    ☐ A @IF<H38>0,H38,0>

    ☐ B @IF[H38>0,H38,0]

    ☐ C @IF(H38>0;H38;0)

    ☐ D @IF(H38>0,H38,0)

9. Which of the following is the correct entry in a cell to convey this message to the program: "If the contents of cell H38 are less than zero, then enter the contents of cell H38 into the current cell; otherwise enter zero":

    ☐ A @IF(H38>0,H38,0)

    ☐ B @IF[H38>0,H38,0]

    ☐ C @IF<H38>0,H38,0)

    ☐ D none of these

10. You have protected your worksheet with the correct global command, and now you want to alter one of the formulae. Before you re-protect the worksheet, you can disable the protection by the keypresses:

    ☐ A /WGPD

    ☐ B /RGPD

    ☐ C /WGPD<Enter>

    ☐ D /RSVP

SESSION 6
Skegness: Accounting Ratios

1. Objectives

At the end of this session you will be able to:

- create a worksheet into which you can enter data and from which seven accounting ratios are automatically calculated
- appreciate how a simple model can be designed
- offset left-aligned labels
- format a range of figures to show only two decimal places
- print your worksheet with a heading
- centre the printed heading
- extend the worksheet by copying ranges of cells
- freeze the borders on the screen
- print borders and a separated range of cells

2. Introduction

In this session, you will create a worksheet which can calculate accounting ratios from data entered into a skeleton Profit & Loss Account and Balance Sheet.

The model is adapted from an example in AFBIS (chapter entitled *Accounting Ratios*).

As in session 5, you will not be given the individual keypresses as you were in the previous sessions. Instead, you are referred to figure 6a which shows the worksheet as it appears on the screen, and figure 6b which shows the same worksheet, but with the formulae required to produce the figures shown in figure 6a. Figure 6b shows column letters, row numbers, labels, values and formulae, from which you should be able to create the worksheet.

Paragraph 3 below describes the model.

Paragraph 4 contains notes on the design of the model.

Paragraph 5 gives notes on creating the worksheet.

Paragraph 6 advises on printing and saving the worksheet.

For the time being you could save your worksheet as you create it with the filename SKEGNESS.

You are advised to read through these paragraphs before starting to create the worksheet from figure 6b.

68

	A	B	C	D	E
1	SKEGNESS				
2	TABLE A: DATA (£000s)	Year ending 31.12.19x3		Year ending 31.12.19x4	
3	PROFIT & LOSS ACCOUNT:	Data:- £	£	Data:- £	£
4	Sales (Turnover)	350		560	
5	Cost of Sales	280		462	
6	Gross Profit	----------	70	----------	98
7	Total Costs	49		56	
8	Net Profit	----------	21	----------	42
9	BALANCE SHEET:				
10	Buildings	35		105	
11	Equipment	70		161	
12	FIXED ASSETS	----------	105	----------	266
13	Stock	56		98	
14	Debtors	35		84	
15	Bank	84		63	
16	CURRENT ASSETS	----------	175	----------	245
17	Creditors	35		28	
18	Dividends	14		35	
19	Overdraft	0		0	
20	CURRENT LIABILITIES	----------	49	----------	63
21	NET CURRENT ASSETS		126		182
22	TOTAL NET ASSETS		231		448
23	Share Capital	140		350	
24	Retained Profit	91		98	
25	CAPITAL EMPLOYED	----------	231	----------	448
26	==				
27	TABLE B: RATIOS	Calcs.	Year ending		Year ending
28	(1) PERFORMANCE RATIOS		31.12.19x3		31.12.19x4
29	[A] Prime Ratio	PBIT x 100			
30	(percentage)	----------	9.09		9.38
31		CE			
32					
33	[B] Profit Margin	PBIT x 100			
34	(percentage)	----------	6.00		7.50
35		Sales			
36					
37	[C] Capital Turnover	Sales			
38	(times)	----------	1.52		1.25
39		CE			
40					
41	[D] Gross Profit	G.P't x 100			
42	(percentage)	----------	20.00		17.50
43		Sales			
44					
45	(2) LIQUIDITY RATIOS				
46	[E] Current Test	CA			
47	(ratio:1)	----------	3.57		3.89
48		CL			
49					
50	[F] Acid Test	CA-Stocks			
51	(ratio:1)	----------	2.43		2.33
52		CL			
53					
54	[G] Debt Collection	Drs. x 365			
55	Period (days)	----------	36.50		54.75
56		Sales			

Figure 6a

69

	A	B	C	D	E
1	SKEGNESS				
2	TABLE A: DATA (£000s)	Year ending 31.12.19x3		Year ending 31.12.19x4	
3	PROFIT & LOSS ACCOUNT:	Data:- £	£	Data:- £	£
4	Sales (Turnover)	350		560	
5	Cost of Sales	280		462	
6	Gross Profit	------------+B4-B5		------------+D4-D5	
7	Total Costs	49		56	
8	Net Profit	------------+C6-B7		------------+E6-D7	
9	BALANCE SHEET:				
10	Buildings	35		105	
11	Equipment	70		161	
12	FIXED ASSETS	------------+B10+B11		------------+D10+D11	
13	Stock	56		98	
14	Debtors	35		84	
15	Bank	84		63	
16	CURRENT ASSETS	------------@SUM(B13..B15)		------------@SUM(D13..D15)	
17	Creditors	35		28	
18	Dividends	14		35	
19	Overdraft	0		0	
20	CURRENT LIABILITIES	------------@SUM(B17..B19)		------------@SUM(D17..D19)	
21	NET CURRENT ASSETS	+C16-C20		+E16-E20	
22	TOTAL NET ASSETS	+C12+C21		+E12+E21	
23	Share Capital	140		350	
24	Retained Profit	91		98	
25	CAPITAL EMPLOYED	------------+B23+B24		------------+D23+D24	
26	===				
27	TABLE B: RATIOS	Calcs.	Year ending		Year ending
28	(1) PERFORMANCE RATIOS		31.12.19x3		31.12.19x4
29	[A] Prime Ratio	PBIT x 100			
30	(percentage)	------------ +C8*100/C25			+E8*100/E25
31		CE			
32					
33	[B] Profit Margin	PBIT x 100			
34	(percentage)	------------ +C8*100/B4			+E8*100/D4
35		Sales			
36					
37	[C] Capital Turnover	Sales			
38	(times)	------------ +B4/C25			+D4/E25
39		CE			
40					
41	[D] Gross Profit	G.P't x 100			
42	(percentage)	------------ +C6*100/B4			+E6*100/D4
43		Sales			
44					
45	(2) LIQUIDITY RATIOS				
46	[E] Current Test	CA			
47	(ratio:1)	------------ +C16/C20			+E16/E20
48		CL			
49					
50	[F] Acid Test	CA-Stocks			
51	(ratio:1)	------------ (C16-B13)/C20			(E16-D13)/E20
52		CL			
53					
54	[G] Debt Collection	Drs. x 365			
55	Period (days)	------------ +B14*365/B4			+D14*365/D4
56		Sales			

Figure 6b

70

3. Description of the model

Skegness is a wholesale trading company. Abbreviated results for two years, 19x3 and 19x4, are set out in Table A of figure 6a, and in Table B seven ratios are calculated from those figures.

The 'Calcs.' column of Table B shows how the ratios are calculated.

PBIT stands for *Profit Before Interest* and *Tax* which is taken here to be *Net Profit* from Table A (line 8)

CE stands for *Capital Employed* (line 25)

G.P't stands for *Gross Profit* (line 6)

CA stands for *Current Assets* (line 16)

CL stands for *Current Liabilities* (line 20)

Drs. stands for *Debtors* (line 14)

Sales stands for *Sales (Turnover)* (line 4)

4. Notes on the design of the model

If you study figure 6b, you will see that this is a print-out containing the formulae used for figure 6a. Both figures 6a and 6b show the cell references: column letters and line numbers. So you should be able to trace the cells to which the formulae refer.

For example, cell C30 contains the formula C8*100/C25. Cell C8 contains the net profit for the first year. This is divided by cell C25, which is the capital employed. The result is multiplied by 100 to give the percentage return (net profit) on capital employed, and this is known as the *Prime Ratio*.

In Table A, columns B and D are the columns into which data are entered. These columns in Table A should stay unprotected. The rest of the worksheet – labels and formulae should be protected. You will be reminded of how to do this in paragraph 5.

The model as it is presented in figures 6a and 6b is a modest one, designed to print out on A4 paper. It may be adequate for you as part of the learning process. However, it could be extended to more years for the same company, or for calculating and comparing the accounting ratios of, say, different companies in the same type of business. Tips on how to do this are given below in paragraph 7.

71

5. Notes on creating the worksheet

COLUMN-WIDTHS

The column-widths used for figure 6a are as follows:

Column A:	22
Column B:	10
Column C:	14
Column D:	10
Column E:	14

Have you forgotten how to do this? (Session 2, paragraph 4) Position the cursor in the appropriate column, and

Press | /WCS |

and type in the column-width, or use the right/left arrow keys, followed by <Enter>

OFFSET TEXT

You will see in column A that some text is offset, e.g in cell A4, the label *Sales (Turnover)* is offset one space to the right of the left-hand side of the cell. To achieve this, simply place the cursor over cell A4, and press the space-bar once, before typing **Sales (Turnover)**. There is no need to type an inverted comma to indicate a left-aligned label before pressing the space-bar. This is done automatically by the program.

Cell A6 contains *Gross Profit* preceded by two spaces, and so on.

TWO DECIMAL PLACES

The ratios shown in table B, columns C and E, are shown in figure 6a with 2 decimal places.

In order to achieve this,

Move the cursor to cell C29

Press | /RFF | (Range, Format, Fixed)

The message appears: *Enter number of decimal places (0..15): 2*

Press | <Enter> | to accept 2 decimal places

Move the cursor to cell C56 using the down-arrow key

Press | <Enter> | and the mode returns to *READY*.

Do the same for the range E29..E56.

PROTECTING LABELS AND FORMULAE

The only cells which you wish to change are in the data-block (Table A), in the ranges B4..B24 and D4..D24.

In case you have forgotten what you learnt in session 5, paragraph 9, here is the procedure:

> Make sure you are in *READY* mode
>
> Move the cursor to cell B4

{123}{VP}   Press | /RU | (Range, Unprotect)

{AEA}   Press | /RLN | (Range, Lock, No)

> Move the cursor to cell B24, and press <Enter>
>
> Follow the same procedure for cells D4..D24.
>
> Press | /WGPE | (Worksheet, Global, Protection, Enable)

6. Printing and saving with a heading

If you followed the suggestion in paragraph 2 above, you have been saving the worksheet with the filename *SKEGNESS*. Retrieve this worksheet if necessary.

If you wish to print out at 10 cpi (characters per inch), assuming that your printer prints at 10 cpi as a default, then here are suggestions for settings. It is a bit of a tight fit to print on 8.25" or 8.5" wide paper, but it is worth trying, if only for experience!

> Press | /PPO | (Print, Printer, Options)

What appears on the screen depends on your program.

> Press | H | (Header)

You are about to enter the heading *ACCOUNTING RATIOS*

> Press | ¦ ACCOUNTING RATIOS | (Header)

The ¦ is the bar which is usually <Shift>+<\>, and is sometimes printed on the key as a broken bar (like --) turned through ninety degrees. This means that the header will be centred. [In order to left-align the header, do not precede the header with a bar. In order to right-align the header, precede it with two bars.]

> Press | <Enter> |

You are returned to the Options menu.

Now set your margins. Refer to session 4, paragraph 8 if you have forgotten the procedure.

Set the Margins as follows:

> Left: 4   Right: 82   Top: 2   Bottom: 2

SETUP can be left blank, since you are using the printer default, though you may care to enter the decimal code for whatever type-style your printer is capable of at 10 cpi

(Refer to session 4, paragraph 7).

Check Page-length, and alter as necessary for your paper type (Refer to session 4, paragraph 6).

Press [Q   ] (Quit) to return to the Print, Printer menu)

Press [R (Range)   ] and specify the range A1..E56.

(Refer to session 4, paragraph 5 if necessary.)

{VP} If you like, you can check your settings fron the Print, Printer menu by pressing S (Status) or /PPS from *READY* mode.

When you are happy with your settings, and while still in the Print, Printer menu,

Press [AGP   ] (Align, Go, Page)

With any luck, you should obtain a good print-out. It is very easy to forget something before pressing Go, and the easiest one to forget is to specify the range. Setup strings are also easy to get wrong. If the printer prints most of the worksheet on the first page, and then proceeds to print something on the next sheet, it is probably due to the setting of the margins.

If you feel that your print-out is rather large for the page, you could try printing it out at 17 cpi. You should refer back to session 4, paragraph 7 if you have forgotten how to do this.

When you find a combination of settings which proves satisfactory, you can save your worksheet with these settings with a new file-name, e.g. if you obtain a good print-out at 17 cpi, and are likely to want to repeat the printout, you could save this version of the worksheet with the filename SKEG17.

7. Extending the worksheet

This paragraph describes how you can extend the worksheet to provide extra columns for analysis, so that it can calculate the ratios for additional years for the same company, or compare the accounting ratios of, say,different companies in the same type of business.

Retrieve your original file *SKEGNESS*

Move the cursor to cell D2

Press [/C   ] (Copy)

Highlight the range D2..E56

Press [<Enter>   ]

Move the cursor to cell F2, and press <Enter>

Note: there is no need to specify more than the top left-hand corner of the destination range.

The range F2..G56 is now a replica of the range D2..E56.

To blank the data cells F4..F5, F7, F10..F11, F13..F15, F17..F19, F23..F24, use /Range, Erase. For example, to erase the data in cells F4..F5:

> Move the cursor to cell F4
>
> Press | /RE<↓> | <Enter>

You could also edit the heading in cell F2 to read *Year ending*:

8. Freezing borders on the screen

If you move the cursor to look at columns F and G, you can no longer see the labels in column A. This is inconvenient, and the problem can be solved by specifying column A so that it will not scroll with the rest of the screen.

> Move the cursor to column B

When you carry out the following keystrokes, the column to the left of column B will be treated as a title {123}{VP} or border {AEA}

{123}{VP}   Press | /WTV | (Worksheet, Titles, Vertical)

{AEA}   Press | /WBV | (Worksheet, Borders, Vertical)

Now move the cursor to column F. You will see that column A stays frozen on the screen.

Save this version of the worksheet with the filename *SKEGVBOR* which is meant to be a mnemonic for SKEGNESS saved with a Vertical BORder.

[Note: If you want to freeze rows above the cursor, use /WTH (Worksheet, Titles, Horizontal) ({AEA} /WBH)

If you want to freeze, for example, row 1 and column A, position the cursor in cell B2, and use /WTB (Worksheet, Titles, Both) ({AEA} use /WBB or /WBH and /WBV separately.)

To unfreeze the borders, you will use /WTC (Worksheet, Titles, Clear) ({AEA} /WBC) in the next paragraph.]

9. Printing borders

If you want to print out, say, columns A, and D..G, here is the procedure:

> Press | /WTC | {AEA} | /WBC |

This clears the border column A which you froze in paragraph 8 above.

> Move the cursor to column A

{123}{VP}   Press | /PPOBC | (Print, Printer, Options, Border, Column)

{AEA}   Press | /PPBC | (Print, Printer, Border, Column)

Press | <Enter> |

IMPORTANT: When specifying the range to be printed, DO NOT include column A, i.e. the border. Choose only the range D1..G56. Otherwise column A will be printed twice.

Now follow the usual procedures for printing.

10. Summary

In this session you should have achieved the objectives set out at the start of this session.

In particular, you should have become acquainted with:

/RFF	Range, Format, Fixed
/PPOH	Print, Printer, Options, Header
/WTV	Worksheet, Titles, Vertical {123}{VP}
/WBV	Worksheet, Borders, Vertical {AEA}
/WTH	Worksheet, Titles, Horizontal {123}{VP}
/WBH	Worksheet, Borders, Horizontal {AEA}
/WTB	Worksheet, Titles, Both {123}{VP}
/WBB	Worksheet, Borders, Both {AEA}
/WTC	Worksheet, Titles, Clear {123}{VP}
/WBC	Worksheet, Borders, Clear {AEA}
/PPOBC	Print,Printer,Options,Border,Column {123}{VP}
/PPBC	Print, Printer, Border, Column {AEA}

11. Activity

Retrieve the worksheet which you saved as *SKEGVBOR* in paragraph 8 above. This version of the worksheet should have column A frozen, and three sets of columns for data and ratio analysis, i.e. B and C, D and E, F and G.

Obtain the report and accounts for a company of your choice for two successive years. The first year should have comparative figures for the previous year, making three years' figures available to you.

Alter the headings in cells B2..G2 appropriately.

[To alter the heading in cell A1 from *SKEGNESS* to the name of your chosen company, you can **either** unfreeze column A, make the alteration and then refreeze it, **or** (not {AEA}) press

76

<F5>, the GoTo key, type A1 and press <Enter>, alter cell A1 in the duplicate copy of column A which appears, and then move the cell pointer to the right until the duplicate column A disappears.]

Enter the appropriate figures from the accounts into the data block (Table A) of the worksheet, and examine the resulting ratios in Table B.

You may have to exercise some ingenuity in entering figures in the Profit and Loss Account, since some published accounts are not very informative. A non-trading company, for example, may have nil 'Cost of Sales'. Also figures from the Balance Sheet may have to be grouped and entered under the limited number of headings in the model. If necessary, alter the headings in column A to broaden their cover.

The Skegness model is a simplified one, and you may feel inspired to redesign it to make it more comprehensive.

12. Objective test ☐ A ☐ B ☑ C ☐ D

This test covers skills acquired in this and previous sessions.

1. In order to widen a single column to 20 characters, the keypresses, after moving the cursor to the required column, are

   ☐ A /WGC20<Enter>
   ☐ B /RC20<Enter>
   ☐ C /WCS20<Enter>
   ☐ D none of these

2. To set a range of cells to show the figures with 3 decimal places, the keypresses required (where [range] means specify the range by typing it in or pointing) are

   ☐ A /RF3F<Enter>[range]<Enter>
   ☐ B /RFF[range]<Enter>3<Enter>
   ☐ C /RFF3<Enter>[range]<Enter>
   ☐ D any of these

3. You wish to print a worksheet with the right-aligned header which reads Table A. Starting from READY mode, the keypresses are

   ☐ A /PPOH | Table A<Enter>
   ☐ B /PPOHTable A<Enter>
   ☐ C /PPOH | | Table A<Enter>
   ☐ D /PPOH\Table A<Enter>

77

4. If you press /WTV (or {AEA} /WBV) while the cursor is on cell C3, the effect on the worksheet will be that

    ☐ A   column C and row 3 are frozen

    ☐ B   rows 1 and 2 are frozen

    ☐ C   columns A and B are frozen

    ☐ D   none of these

5. If you press /WTH (or {AEA} /WBH) while the cursor is on cell C2, the effect on the worksheet will be that

    ☐ A   row 1 is frozen

    ☐ B   column A is frozen

    ☐ C   rows 1 and 2 are frozen

    ☐ D   columns A and B are frozen

6. If you have frozen some columns and/or rows, and you now want to unfreeze them, the keypresses are (for {AEA} read B for T)

    ☐ A   /WGCT

    ☐ B   /WGT

    ☐ C   /WGTC

    ☐ D   /WTC

7. You have just wasted a lot of continuous paper due to setting your right-margin at 12 instead of 82. To correct this before pressing Go again, the keystrokes from READY mode are

    ☐ A   /PPOMR82<Enter>Q

    ☐ B   /PPOMR<Enter>82<Enter>Q

    ☐ C   /PPMR82<Enter>Q

    ☐ D   /PPOMR82<Enter>

8. The labels in cells C2..H2 have been entered at the default (left-aligned). You wish the centre them. The keypresses required, where [range] means specify the range by typing it in or pointing), are (for {AEA} read P for L)

    ☐ A   /WGLC[Range]<Enter>

    ☐ B   /RCL[Range]<Enter>

    ☐ C   /RLC[range]<Enter>

    ☐ D   /LGOC[range]<Enter>

9. You have entered a rude word in cell X99. You wish to erase it before anyone sees it. The best way to do so, with the cursor on cell X99, is to press

☐ A /RE<Enter>

☐ B /RD<Enter>

☐ C /Q<Enter>

☐ D /WE<Enter>

10. You are half-way through working on a worksheet, and you want a cup of coffee. You have saved your worksheet with a suitable name several times so far. Before going for your coffee, you should press

☐ A /FSR<Enter>

☐ B /FS<Enter>R

☐ C /FS<Enter>

☐ D /TTFN<Enter>

SESSION 7
Creating Graphs

1. Objectives

At the end of this session, you will be able to:

- ❏ create a worksheet in a format suitable for creating graphs
- ❏ create some formulae which conform to the requirements of the data
- ❏ define the necessary set-up for a graph
- ❏ enhance a graph with titles and legends
- ❏ name a graph
- ❏ save a graph ready for printing
- ❏ create bar, line, stacked-bar and pie graphs

2. Introduction

In this session, you will create a worksheet which sets out the budgeted sales data for a bicycle manufacturing company in a table of suitable format, and then produce graphs from that table which improve the presentation and facilitate interpretation of the data.

As in sessions 5 and 6, you will not be given all the individual keypresses. Instead, you are referred to figure 7a which shows the worksheet as it appears on the screen, and figure 7b which shows the same worksheet, but with the formulae required to produce the figures shown in figure 7a. Figure 7b shows column letters, row numbers, labels, values and formulae, from which you should be able to create the worksheet.

Paragraph 3 below sets the problem and describes the model.

Paragraph 4 contains notes on the design of the model.

Paragraph 5 gives notes on creating the worksheet.

Paragraphs 6, 7, 8 and 9 show you how to define, enhance, name and save a bar graph based on the worksheet.

Paragraphs 10, 11 and 12 show you how to do the same for line, stacked-bar and pie graphs.

Figure 7a

	A	B	C	D	E	F
1			The Zed Bicycle Company			
2			Budgeted Sales for Next Year			
3						
4	Qtr:-		Spring	Summer	Autumn	Winter	Totals
5		--------	--------	--------	--------	--------	--------
6	Model:-		£	£	£	£	£
7	Alpha		80,000	96,000	115,200	138,240	429,440
8	Beta		90,000	99,000	108,900	119,790	417,690
9	Gamma		80,000	80,000	90,000	90,000	340,000
10	Delta		60,000	54,000	58,600	52,740	225,340
11		--------	--------	--------	--------	--------	--------
12	Totals		310,000	329,000	372,700	400,770	1,412,470
13		===					

Figure 7b

	A	B	C	D	E	F
1			The Zed Bicycle Company			
2			Budgeted Sales for Next Year			
3						
4	Qtr:-	Spring	Summer	Autumn	Winter	Totals
5		--------	--------	--------	--------	--------
6	Model:-	£	£	£	£	£
7	Alpha	80000	+B7*1.2	+C7*1.2	+D7*1.2	@SUM(B7..E7)
8	Beta	90000	+B8*1.1	+C8*1.1	+D8*1.1	@SUM(B8..E8)
9	Gamma	80000	+B9	+C9+10000	+D9	@SUM(B9..E9)
10	Delta	60000	+B10*.9	(C10*.9)+10000	+D10*.9	@SUM(B10..E10)
11		--------	--------	--------	--------	--------
12	Totals	@SUM(B7..B10)	@SUM(C7..C10)	@SUM(D7..D10)	@SUM(E7..E10)	@SUM(F7..F10)
13		===				

That should be enough for this session, and in session 8 you will print out the graphs created and saved in this session.

3. Description of the model

The ZED BICYCLE COMPANY manufactures four models of bicycle: the Alpha, Beta, Gamma and Delta. The sales manager has just completed his budgeted sales figures for next year, which, for budget purposes, is sub-analysed into spring, summer, autumn and winter quarters.

For the spring quarter, he anticipates sales as follows:

	£
Alpha	80,000
Beta	90,000
Gamma	80,000
Delta	60,000

He also anticipates growth of sales in each quarter over the previous quarter, as follows:

Alpha	20%
Beta	10%
Gamma	nil
Delta	-10%

In view of the nil growth rate for the Gamma, and the negative growth rate for the Delta, he plans to spend some money on advertising for these two models. As a result of that advertising, he expects that sales of each model will increase by £10,000 in the autumn quarter, on top of the originally budgeted sales figures. In the winter quarter, he expects sales to change by the usual growth rates (nil and -10%) over the autumn quarter's sales which include the additional sales in the autumn quarter resulting from the advertising.

These expectations have been translated into a table, which is shown in figure 7a. In figure 7b, you will see the budgeted values for the spring quarter, and the formulae required to calculate the budgeted sales for the last three quarters of next year.

4. Notes on the design of the model

If you study figure 7b, you will see that this is a print-out containing the formulae used for figure 7a. Both figures 7a and 7b show the cell references: column letters and row numbers. So you should be able to trace the cells to which the formulae refer.

Cells B7..B10 contain the values for the budgeted sales for the spring quarter. The range C7..E10 contains formulae directly or indirectly derived from the range B7..B10. Cells C7..C10 calculate the sales for the summer quarter, using the values in cells B7..B10 multiplied by the growth factors supplied by the sales manager. Note that cell C9 has a nil growth factor, and therefore simply has the entry +B9. Cells D7..D10 use the resulting values in cells C7..C10, again multiplied by the same growth factors. However cells D9 and D10 each have £10,000 added, for the extra budgeted sales arising from additional advertising. Cells E7..E10 use the resulting values in cells D7..D10 (including the extra £10,000s), multiplied by the growth factors.

All these formulae are designed to conform with the information supplied by the sales manager.

Cells F7..F10 and B12..F12 contain formulae which total the respective rows and columns.

5. Notes on creating the worksheet

The following notes refer to figure 7a.

COLUMN-WIDTH

Before entering the labels, values and formulae, it is suggested that you set the global column-width at 11:

Press | `/WGC11<Enter>`

Comments on suitable column-widths and printer option settings are given below (at the end of this paragraph).

ENTERING THE LABELS

The labels in rows 1 and 2 are in cells C1 and C2. The label in C1 is preceded by three spaces. Starting a label with a space does not require a ' to be typed.

Cells A4..F4 and B6..F6 (Fig 7a) are right-aligned.

Cells A6..A10 and A12 and also B6.. F6 (Fig 7b) are left-aligned.

[If you find that the £ signs in cells B6..F6 do not print out, try substituting a # sign. This depends on the your program and printer. This was mentioned in session 4, paragraph 5, and you may have solved the problem then.]

ENTERING THE VALUES

Cells B7..B10 contain the values. Do not forget to enter these values **without** commas or £ sign preceding them.

To obtain the commas,

Press `/WGF,0<Enter>`

[Note: to obtain £ signs in front of every figure (values as well as figures resulting from formulae), you would press: **/WGFC0<Enter>**. To cancel both commas and £ signs, you would press **/WGFG**.]

ENTERING THE FORMULAE

Cell C7: this contains the formula +B7*1.2. To enter this, you could type it in as shown, or you could try:

Press `+b7*120%<Enter>`

Note: some keyboards have a very convenient set of keys at the top right-hand side, which duplicate the keys for:

/ * – +

These are convenient for entering formulae, since the <Shift> key is not required, and they are easy to locate.

When you have entered cells C7..C10, copy this range to the range D7..E10. You will see that the formulae are all relative to the cell to the left, which is what we require in this instance.

Cells D9 and D10 only: Edit (using the <F2> key) the formulae and add +10000 after the existing formulae in each cell.

Cell D9: The brackets are not strictly necessary; * is calculated before +.

Cell B12: Don't forget that you can **point** to cells B7..B10 when entering the formula *@SUM(B7..B10)*. If you have forgotten how to do this, refer back to session 3, paragraph 8). You can use the same technique for cell F7.

Cell F7 can be copied to cells F8..F10, and cell B12 can be copied to cells C12..F12.

COLUMN-WIDTHS AND PRINTER SETTINGS

The global column-width chosen for figure 7a is the global column-width of 11. This could be less, but 11 was chosen because there is adequate room for printing out at 10 cpi on A4 paper at this width, and the wider columns give a less cramped appearance.

If you want to print out this worksheet later, the following settings are suggested for 10 cpi: ML 4, MR 80, MT 10, MB2.

You could set them now, before you forget, using /PPOM.

[Don't forget to define the Range, and to enter any Setup string required to print at 10 cpi.]

When you have defined satisfactory print options, save the worksheet as *ZED7A*.

Figure 7b used /WGFT (Worksheet, Global, Format, Text) to display all the formulae. The global column-width chosen is 17. This, again, could be less, but the print-out at 17 cpi is less cramped with the slightly wider columns.

Suggested settings for margins, to print at 17 cpi on A4 paper, are: ML 10, MR 132, MT10, MB 2

You may feel that the labels in the range B4..F4 would look better left-aligned:

Use   `/RLLB4.F4<Enter>`   (AEA)   `/RPLB4.F4<Enter>`

This version of the worksheet could be saved as *ZED7B*.

6. Defining the bar graph

Retrieve the worksheet which you saved as ZED7A.

From *READY* mode, press   `/GTB`   (Graph, Type, Bar)

[You are advised, as usual, to proceed slowly, observing the changes to the menus in the control panel, or drop-down menus.]

You have now selected a bar type of graph, and you are returned to the main graph menu.

Press   `A`

Move the cursor to cell B7

Press   `.`   (a full stop)

Move the cursor to cell E7, and press <Enter>

You have now defined graph range A for the Alpha bicycle. There are 6 graph ranges available, A – F inclusive. You are going to use the first four of these, A – D inclusive, covering the four models of bicycle.

From now on, when you see [range] in these instructions, define the range following [range]. For example, the instructions for defining the A range above will be shown as:

Press | A [range]B7..E7 <Enter> |

You can, of course, type the range in (type b7.e7), if you prefer doing so to pointing.

Press | B [range]B8..E8 <Enter> |

Press | C [range]B9..E9 <Enter> |

Press | D [range]B10..E10 <Enter> |

You should now be back at the graph menu, and you should see View in the control panel or drop-down menu.

{AEA}   Do not view yet, until you have defined the X range.

           Go to the start of the next paragraph.

{123}{VP}   Press | V | (View)

A bar graph should appear on your monitor (assuming you have a graphics card and a monitor which supports graphics).

[This graph should be similar to figure 8a or 8b (in session 8), but without most of the words.]

Press | <Esc> | to return to the graph menu.

7. Enhancing the bar graph

Press | X [range]B4.E4 | <Enter>

This defines the X range (Spring..Winter)

Press | V | to view the addition of the labels added to the X axis data points.

Press | <Esc> | to return to the graph menu.

Press | O | (Options)

You will use the *Legend* and *Titles* options in this Option sub-menu.

Press | LA | (Legend, A range)

{123}{VP}	Press	`\A7`	<Enter>

{AEA}	Type	`Alpha`	<Enter>

{123}{VP}   Cell A7 contains the legend *Alpha* and typing in \A7 against the prompt saved you having to type in Alpha.

Note: More characters can be displayed by this cell-reference method than by typing in a legend. The numbers vary between programs.

{123}{VP}	Press	`LB\A8`	<Enter>

{AEA}	Type	`LBBeta`	<Enter>

{123}{VP}	Press	`LC\A9`	<Enter>

{AEA}	Type	`LCGamma`	<Enter>

{123}{VP}	Press	`LD\A10`	<Enter>

{AEA}	Type	`LDDelta`	<Enter>

Press `QV` (Quit, View) to view the graph with legends added.

Press `<Esc>` to return to the main graph menu.

Press `OT` (Options, Titles)

You are now going to specify titles.

{123}{VP}	Press	`F\C1`	<Enter>

{AEA}	Type	`FThe ZED Bicycle Company`	<Enter>

This enters *The ZED Bicycle Company* at the top of the graph.

{123}{VP}	Press	`TS\C2`	<Enter>

{AEA}	Type	`SBudgeted Sales for Next Year`	<Enter>

This enters *Budgeted Sales for Next Year* on the second line.

Press {123}{VP} `TX`   {AEA} `X`

Type `Budgeted Sales per Quarter`

86

Press	<Enter>

Press {123}{VP}	TY	{AEA}	Y

Type	Pounds

Press	<Enter>

Press {123}{VP}	QV	(Quit, View)	{AEA}	QQV

You should now see the graph with legends and titles on your monitor. You can check for mistakes, and repeat any sequence of keystrokes necessary to correct them.

8. Naming the bar graph

Your program can maintain only one set of graph definitions at any time, unless you have given a name to each set of definitions.

Return to the main graph menu.

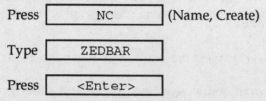

Press	NC	(Name, Create)

Type	ZEDBAR

Press	<Enter>

The worksheet has already been saved with the file name *ZED7A* (and *ZED7B*, if you saved the /WGFT version at the end of paragraph 5). Now save it again with the name *ZEDGRAPH* :-

Press	Q/FS

Type	ZEDGRAPH

9. Saving the bar graph

{AEA} has a different method of printing, which is shown as Plot in the Graphics menu. Some of this paragraph (9) is therefore inapplicable. Details of how to use the Plot sub-menu will be given in the next session. However, you should work through paragraphs 9, 10, 11 and 12 of this session (session 7), but you should ignore the Save commands, where they are marked: {not AEA}.

To save the graphic image for printing, it should be saved with a separate file-name. In the next three paragraphs, you will be creating a line graph, stacked-bar graph and pie graph, and each one should be named and saved separately if you want to print them later.

So far you have defined and named a bar graph for the Zed Bicycle Company sales budget. Now you will save it in what is known as a *PIC* file, i.e. one with a *.PIC* extension, in this case *ZEDBAR.PIC*.

You should now be back at the main menu (READY mode).

Type ▭ /GNU ▭ (Graph, Name, Use)

The name *ZEDBAR* should appear, and since it is the only named graph so far, it should be high-lighted.

Press ▭ <Enter> ▭ to accept it

You have now made *ZEDBAR* the current graph, and the graph should appear on the monitor as a check that you have the correct graph current.

Press ▭ <Esc> ▭ to get back to the graph menu.

{notAEA}   Press ▭ S ▭ (Save)

{notAEA}   Type ▭ ZEDBAR ▭

{notAEA}   Press ▭ <Enter> ▭

{notAEA} You have now created a file called *ZEDBAR.PIC* and saved it to disk.

In the next session (Session 8) you will print out your *ZEDBAR* graph. Before doing so, (unless you cannot wait) you can create, name and save some more graphs, based on the same data.

10. Line graph

You may feel competent now to create, name and save a line graph (and other graphs) without any further help. If so, carry on! If not, carry out the abbreviated instructions in this paragraph (and the next two paragraphs for stacked-bar and pie graphs).

You should still be in the main graph menu.

Press ▭ TLV ▭ (Type, Line, View)

Press ▭ <Esc>NC ▭ (Name, Create)

Type ▭ ZEDLINE ▭ <Enter>

Press ▭ NU ▭ (Name, Use)

Highlight ▭ ZEDLINE ▭ <Enter> <Esc>

{notAEA}   Press ▭ S ▭ (Save)

{notAEA}   Type ▭ ZEDLINE ▭ <Enter>

11. Stacked-bar graph

Press <code>   TSV   </code> (Type, Stacked-bar, View)

Press <code>   <Esc> NC   </code> (Name, Create)

Press <code>   ZEDSTACK   </code> <Enter>

Press <code>   NU   </code> (Name, Use)

Highlight <code>   ZEDSTACK   </code> <Enter> <Esc>

{notAEA}   Press <code>   S   </code> (Save)

{notAEA}   Type <code>   ZEDSTACK   </code> <Enter>

12. Pie Graph

Press <code>   TP   </code> (Type, Pie)

You will now have to alter the definitions slightly, since the A range is set for cells B7..E7, which is for the Alpha bicycle, and you need total sales for each quarter.

Press <code>   A   </code>

The range B7..E7 is highlighted.

Press <code>   <Esc>   </code>

Move the cursor to cell B12, type a full-stop, move the cursor to cell E12 and press <Enter>

The range already set for X is B4..E4, which is what you require.

Press <code>   V   </code> (View), and check that this is the graph you require.

Press <code>   <Esc>   </code> to return to the graph menu

Press <code>   NC   </code> (Name, Create)

Type <code>   ZEDPIE   </code> <Enter>

Press <code>   NU   </code> (Name, Use)

Highlight <code>   ZEDPIE   </code> <Enter> <Esc>

{notAEA}   Press <code>   S   </code> (Save)

{notAEA}   Type | ZEDPIE | <Enter>

Do not forget to save the current ZEDGRAPH worksheet before you end this session:

Press | Q/FS<Enter>R |

13. Summary

In this session you should have achieved the objectives set out at the start of this session.

In particular, you should have become acquainted with:

/WGF,0	Worksheet, Global, Format, Comma, Zero
/WGFC0	Worksheet, Global, Format, Currency, Zero
/WGFG	Worksheet, Global, Format, General
/ * - +	Duplicate keys for entering formulae
/GTB	Graph, Type, Bar
/GTL	Graph, Type, Line
/GTS	Graph, Type, Stacked-bar
/GTP	Graph, Type, Pie
/GX	Graph, X-range
/GA	Graph, A-range
/GOL	Graph, Options, Legend
/GOT	Graph, Options, Titles
/GNC	Graph, Name, Create
/GNU	Graph, Name, Use
/GS	Graph, Save (not{AEA})

14. Activity

Invent some budgeted data for an organisation for three or four activities or products, for a period of six separate months.

Create (and save!) a worksheet which conforms with your data.

Define, enhance, name and save bar, line, stacked-bar and pie graphs created from the data in your worksheet.

15. Objective test ☐ A ☐ B ☑ C ☐ D

1. To enter £7,000 into a cell, you should type, before pressing <Enter>

    ☐ A 7000

    ☐ B 7,000

    ☐ C £7,000

    ☐ D any of these

2. With a value of 7000 entered into a cell, the keypresses required to show 7,000 in the cell, before pressing <Enter> are

    ☐ A /WFG,

    ☐ B /WFG,0

    ☐ C /WF,0

    ☐ D /WGF,0

3. To enter a formula into cell A3 which increases the value in cell A1 by 20%, the formula to be entered is

    ☐ A +a1x120%

    ☐ B +A1+20%

    ☐ C +A1*1.2

    ☐ D +A1*20%

4. To define a bar graph, the initial keystrokes from READY mode are

    ☐ A /GTB

    ☐ B /WGTB

    ☐ C /WGB

    ☐ D /GB

5. From READY mode, legends can be added to a graph for the A range after the keypresses:

    ☐ A /WGLA

    ☐ B /GTLA

    ☐ C /GOLA

    ☐ D /GTOLA

91

6. From READY mode, titles can be added to a graph for the X-Axis after the keypresses:

   ☐ A /GTX

   ☐ B /GOTX

   ☐ C /GTOX

   ☐ D /WGTOX

7. Once you have defined and enhanced a graph, you should name it before defining and enhancing another graph from the same data. You can do this by the following keypresses from READY mode:

   ☐ A /GNC

   ☐ B /GONC

   ☐ C /GTNC

   ☐ D /ONC

8. You have named a graph with the name CHOCBAR. To make this the current graph, you should press, before you highlight CHOCBAR and press <Enter>, starting from the Graph menu:

   ☐ A ONU

   ☐ B NU<Enter>

   ☐ C NU

   ☐ D NC<Enter>

9. You have finished defining, enhancing and naming a bar graph. You now want to view a line graph from the same data. From the graph menu, the keypresses are:

   ☐ A TLV

   ☐ B OTLV

   ☐ C OTVL

   ☐ D none of these

10. A graph is on the screen, and you want to get rid of it. So you press:

   ☐ A <Space-bar>

   ☐ B <Enter>

   ☐ C either A or B

   ☐ D neither A nor B

SESSION 8
Printing Graphs

1. Objectives

At the end of this session (assuming you have a graphics printer) you will be able to:

- ❑ print out any of the graphs which you created in session 7
- ❑ appreciate the capabilities of the printing facilities available for your particular spreadsheet program

2. Introduction

In session 7, you created and named four types of graph.

Also {123}{VP} you saved them with the file-names:

> ZEDBAR.PIC
> ZEDLINE.PIC
> ZEDSTACK.PIC
> ZEDPIE.PIC

In this session you will learn how to print them out on paper.

It is important to note that you must have a graphics printer to print graphs.

The programs used in this book have different graph-printing support. Refer to the paragraphs below which are relevant to your program.

Program	Paragraphs
{123}	3, 4, 5
{VP}	6
(AEA)	7

3. {123} Acessing Printgraph

In session 1 , you were shown how to get a blank worksheet by going through the Lotus Access System Screen. This screen shows when you type *Lotus* at the C:> or C:\123> prompt (once you have changed to the *1-2-3* sub-directory). So far you have chosen only *1-2-3* from the menu to obtain a blank worksheet. The choice to the right of 1-2-3 is *PrintGraph,* and this is a separate program which you will use to print your graphs.

[If you want to go straight to a blank worksheet, without going through the Access screen, you can type **123 <Enter>** at the prompt. However, if you then want to use the PrintGraph program, you have to Quit the 1-2-3 program, and (assuming you are still in your 1-2-3 sub-directory) type **Printgraph** at the C:> prompt.]

Start this session by accessing a blank worksheet by typing Lotus at the prompt, and then press <Enter> with the high-light over *1-2-3*.

Refresh your memory of the four graphs you created in session 7 by looking at them on your monitor.

Press | /FR |

Press | <F3> | to list the files you have created

Move the cursor to *ZEDGRAPH* and press <Enter>

Press | /GNU | (Graph, Name, Use)

Select the graph you want to see on screen with the cursor, and press <Enter>

To view another graph,

Press | <Esc> NU | (Name, Use)

Select the next graph with the cursor.

Press | <Enter> |

> **Tip:** After viewing one graph and pressing **<Esc>**, the cursor will already be on *Name*. Press <Enter> and the cursor will be on Use. Press **<Enter>** again, and you can now select the graph you want. Also, pressing other keys besides **<Esc>** works to take you from the graph on the screen back to the main graph menu. So, when you have finished viewing one graph, and want to view another, you could simply press **<Enter>** three times, to achieve the same result as pressing **<Esc>NU**. Try it and see. As you use spreadsheets, look out for short-cuts!

Practise viewing the graphs until the process becomes easy.

4. {123} Preparing Printgraph

Before you print your graphs, it is necessary to check and, if necessary, change the printgraph settings, so that your graphs print out correctly.

After viewing your last graph, press <Enter> to return you to the main graph menu.

Press | Q | (Quit)

This takes you back to READY mode

Press | /QY | (Quit, Yes)

You should now be back at the 1-2-3 Access System Screen. If not, see paragraph 2 above.

Move the cursor to *PrintGraph* and press <Enter>

You will see a menu, with a status screen below.

Move the cursor to *Settings* and press <Enter>

Move the cursor to *Hardware* and press <Enter>

You will see a menu with selections corresponding to the headings under *HARDWARE SETUP* in the status screen.

Check each item to see if it is correct.

Graphs Directory should show the drive and directory where your graphs were saved, i.e. the same directory as *ZEDGRAPH*. If the directory shown is incorrect, choose *Graphs-Directory* in the menu and press <Enter>; then type in the correct drive and directory, such as *A:* or *B:* or *C:\123*.

Fonts Directory should show the drive and directory where your font (.FNT) files are. For example, if your font files are in the subdirectory 123 of drive C:, the entry should be C:\123. If the entry is incorrect, choose *Fonts-Directory*, press <Enter> and type in the correct drive and directory.

Interface refers to the way your printer is connected to your computer. Do not make any changes unless you understand fully your type of printer. The most common setting is Parallel 1, which is the first option when you choose *Interface* from the menu. Your printer manual should tell you what interface you need. Other options can be read from the control panel by moving the right- or left- arrow keys. Do NOT press <Enter> unless you need to make a change. Press <Esc> to keep the setting on the status screen as it is.

Printer Type: Check that your printer is shown in the status screen. If not, choose *Printer* from the menu. Follow the instructions on the screen. [If no options are displayed, or if your printer is not listed, you will have to return to the Install program.]

Paper Size: Alter width and length if necessary. Follow the instructions on the screen.

Press [Q] (Quit)

Press [S] (Save) if you want to save your current settings for future sessions

Press [Q] (Quit) to return to the main menu

5. {123} Printing your graphs

At last! It may seem tedious to have to check the settings as described in the previous paragraph, but, once the settings have been saved, you will not have to do it again unless you make a change, e.g. to your printer or paper size.

Press [I] (Image-Select)

You should see a list of your four graph (.PIC) files, with the date and time you saved them, and also the file sizes.

Move the cursor (if necessary) to *ZEDBAR*

Press [<Spacebar>]

This marks *ZEDBAR* with a hash sign

Press [<Enter>] to select it

You are returned to the main menu, and you will see *ZEDBAR* listed under *GRAPH IMAGES SELECTED*

Press [AGP] (Align, Go, Page)

This is the same procedure as you learnt when printing your worksheet in session 4.

The *ZEDBAR* graph should print out and the paper (if continuous) should advance to the top of the next page.

Your graph should look similar to Figure 8a.

[If you want to view your graphs as a check before you print them (or to look at them in any case) you can do this when you select *Image-Select* by high-lighting the file you want to view and pressing <F10>. Press <Esc> to return to the *Image-Select* screen.]

Next, to print out *ZEDLINE* :

Press [I] (Image-Select)

Move the cursor to *ZEDBAR* and press **<Spacebar>**

This turns the mark (#) off

Move the cursor to *ZEDLINE* and press **<Spacebar>**

This turns the mark (#) on

Press [<Enter>] to select the marked graph and returnyou to the main
menu.

You will see *ZEDLINE* listed under *GRAPH IMAGES SELECTED*

Press [AGP] (Align, Go, Page)

The *ZEDLINE* graph should print out and the paper (if continuous) should advance to the top of the next page.

Finally you will print out *ZEDPIE* and *ZEDSTACK* in one operation.

Press [I] (Image-Select)

Figure 8a

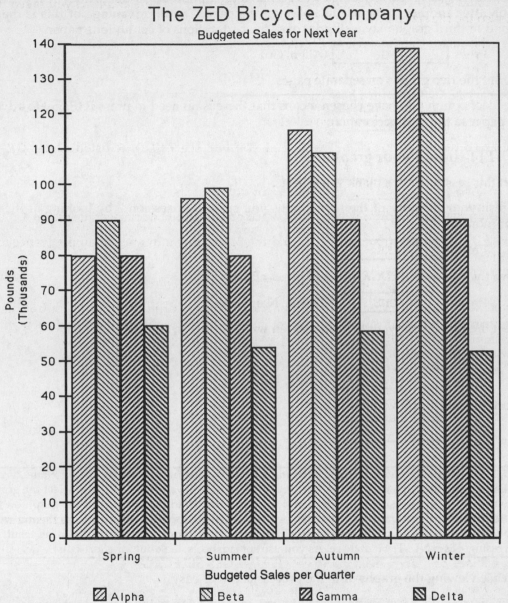

The ZED Bicycle Company
Budgeted Sales for Next Year

Cancel the mark against *ZEDLINE*, and mark *ZEDPIE* and *ZEDSTACK* using the **<Spacebar>**.

Press | <Enter> |

Press | SAEYQQ | (Settings, Action, Eject, Yes, Quit, Quit)

97

By setting *ACTION OPTIONS Eject* to *Yes* the printer will advance to the next page when each individual graph is printed. If you leave the option at *No* the printer will print one graph after another using all the space on the page. The disadvantage of this is that the second or third graph may well print over the perforations of continuous paper.

Press | AG | (Align, Go)

to print the two graphs on separate pages.

The Eject option you have chosen means that there is no need to press P (Page) to advance the paper to the next perforation.

6. {VP} Printing your graphs

Start this session with a blank worksheet.

Refresh your memory of the four graphs you created in session 7 by looking at them on your monitor.

Press | /FR |

Move the cursor to *ZEDGRAPH* and press <Enter>

Press | /GNU | (Graph, Name, Use)

Select the graph you want to see on screen with the cursor, and press <Enter>

To view another graph,

Press | <Esc> NU | (Name, Use)

Select the next graph with the cursor.

Press | <Enter> |

Tip: After viewing one graph and pressing <Esc>, the cursor will already be on Name. Press <Enter> and the cursor will be on Use. Press <Enter> again, and you can now select the graph you want. Also, pressing other keys besides <Esc> works to take you from the graph on the screen back to the main graph menu. So, when you have finished viewing one graph, and want to view another, you could simply press <Enter> three times, to achieve the same result as pressing <Esc>NU. Try it and see. As you use spreadsheets, look out for short-cuts!

Practise viewing the graphs until the process becomes easy.

After viewing your last graph, press <Enter> to return you to the main graph menu.

Selecting **V** (View) from the main graph menu enables you to view the current (named with Name, Use) graph only.

You can also view your graphs which you saved in *.PIC* files. Select *Look* from the main graph menu, and your *.PIC* are listed for you to select for viewing.

[A current graph (after Name, Use) can also be viewed from *READY* mode by pressing <F10>.]

Printing with {VP} is simple:

From the Graph menu:

Press | NU | (Name, Use)

Highlight the graph name you wish to make current

Press | <Enter> |

The graph appears on the screen.

Press | <Esc> | to return you to the main graph menu.

Press | P | (Print)

The graph appears on the screen and the printer prints the current graph sideways.

[You may possibly be able to print a graph while it is displayed on your monitor after pressing (from *READY* mode) /GV (Graph, View) or /GL (Graph, Look) or <F10>, by pressing **<Shift>+<PrintScreen>**. You may waste paper trying!]

Once you have saved your graphs in a *.PIC* file, it can by readby other graphics programs for more elaborate print-outs.

If you have time, you could experiment by printing out your other graphs.

7. {AEA} Printing your graphs

Start this session with a blank worksheet.

Refresh your memory of the four graphs you created in session 7 by looking at them on your monitor.

Press | /FR |

Move the cursor to *ZEDGRAPH* and press **<Enter>**

Press | /GNU | (Graphics, Name, Use)

Select the graph you want to see on screen with the cursor, and press **<Enter>**

To view another graph,

Press | <Esc> NU | (Name, Use)

Select the next graph with the cursor.

Press | <Enter> |

> *Tip:* After viewing one graph and pressing **<Esc>**, the cursor will already be on *Name*. Press **<Enter>** and the cursor will be on Use. Press **<Enter>** again, and you can now select the graph you want. Also, pressing other keys besides **<Esc>** works to take you from the graph on the screen back to the main graph menu. So, when you have finished viewing one graph, and want to view another, you could simply press **<Enter>** three times, to achieve the same result as pressing **<Esc>NU**. Try it and see. As you use spreadsheets, look out for short-cuts!

Practise viewing the graphs until the process becomes easy.

After viewing your last graph, press **<Enter>** to return you to the main graphics menu.

Selecting **V** (View) from the main graph menu enables you to view the current (named with Name, Use) graph only.

[A current graph (after Name, Use) can also be viewed from *READY* mode by pressing **<F10>**.]

Printing with {AEA} is simple:

From the Graphics menu:

Press | NU | (Name, Use)

Highlight the graph name *ZEDBAR* to make it current

Press | <Enter> |

The graph appears on the screen.

Press | <Esc> | to return you to the main graph menu.

Press | P | (Plot)

This enters the *Graphics Plot* menu, from which a printed copy of the current graph can be produced.

The menu choices are:

Image	Density	Hardware	Paper	Orient	Eject	GO	Quit
High	Low	PIC	Height	Portrait			
Wide	High	LASER	Width	Landscape			
Top		FX/MX	Quit				
Bottom		24-PIN					
Left							
Quit							

Your menus may differ slightly from the above, depending on your version of the program. Many of these options are not available in version 3.

Full details of these menu items are given in the manual under *GRAPHICS COMMAND SUMMARY*.

You will now print out your *ZEDBAR* graph, using some of the choices available.

Press `        IH        ` (Image, High)

The height of the graph is to be set in hundredths of an inch. So to make the graph 4 inches high, accept the default value of 400 by pressing **<Enter>**, or alter it to 400 if the default has changed.

Press `        W        ` (Wide)

Accept the default value of 600 by pressing **<Enter>**, or alter it to 600 if the default has changed.

Press `        T        ` (Top)

Type `        50        ` (to set at half an inch)

Press `        B        ` (Bottom)

Type `        100        ` (to set at one inch, because the legends and titles need this space)

Press `        L        ` (Left)

Type `        100        ` (to set left margin at one inch)

Press `        Q        ` (Quit, to return to the Graphics menu)

Press `        D        ` (Density)

Choose *Low* or *High*. High gives a better print-out but takes longer to print. Choose L for a faster first-time printout, in case you want to alter the settings before producing a final high-quality print-out.

Press `        H        ` (Hardware)

PIC sends the output to a *.PIC* file (which is a file which can be read by some other graphics and word-processing programs). If you remember, in session 7, you could not do this at that stage.

Your choice of one of the other three menu items depends on what printer you are using. *FX/MX* is for a 9-pin Epson or compatible dot-matrix printer.

Move the cursor to your type of printer

Press `   <Enter>   `

Press `        P        ` (Paper)

The defaults are probably for 1100 x 800 (11" x 8") paper, but you should change this for A4 paper to 1166 x 825.

Press `    H    ` and type in height required.   Press `  <Enter>  `

Press `    W    ` and type in width required.   Press `  <Enter>  `

Press `    Q    ` (Quit)

Press `    O    ` (Orient)

Press `    P    ` (Portrait)   Press `  <Enter>  `

If you are happy that you have set-up your print-out correctly,

Press `    G    ` (Go)

The mode indicator at the top of the screen will flash *WAIT*. The screen will read *Plotting...Press ESC to Stop* , and the progress of the printing is shown below as a percentage.

The speed of printing will vary with your choice of high or low density.

When the printing has stopped, move the paper to the top of the next sheet. You printer controls (line feed) may be better than pressing *Eject* which sometimes moves to the top of the next but one sheet of continuous paper.

Your graph should look similar to Figure 8b.

Press `    QQ    ` (Quit, Quit) to return to READY! mode.

If you have time, you could experiment by printing out your other graphs.

8. Summary

In this session you should have achieved the objectives set out at the start of this session.

The basic principles of printing graphs with the various programs are:

- define, enhance, name and {notAEA} save individual graphs

{123}
- access the PrintGraph program
- check the PrintGraph settings
- choose Image-Select and your graph PIC file
- Align, Go, Page

{VP}
- /GNU (Graph, Name, Use)
- Select your graph
- P for Print

{AEA}
- /GNU (Graphics, Name, Use)
- Select your graph
- P for Plot
- check and alter Plot menu settings
- G for Go

Figure 8b

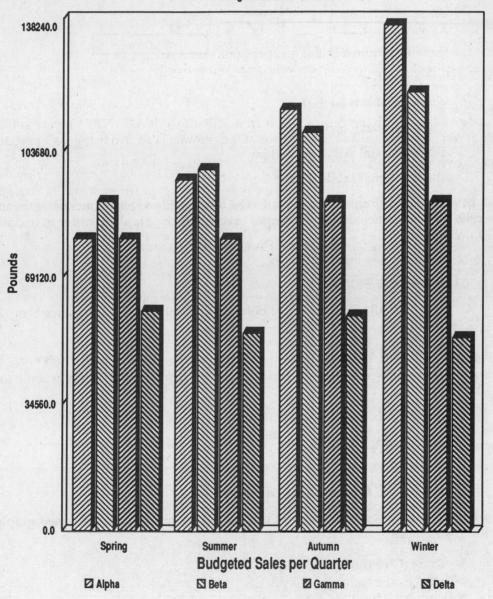

9. Activity

Print out the graphs which you created during the activity of the last session (Session 7, paragraph 14).

Try not to waste too much paper doing so! Check your settings carefully.

10. Objective test ☐ A ☐ B ☑ C ☐ D

This test covers skills acquired in this and previous sessions.

1. The X-axis in a graph is

   ☐ A   the vertical axis on the left

   ☐ B   the vertical axis on the right

   ☐ C   the horizontal axis at the bottom

   ☐ D   the horizontal axis at the top

2. You have created a graph and named it. You now decide to alter some of the values in the cells which are included in the ranges covered by the graph. In order to update the graph, you must

   ☐ A   redefine the ranges A, B, C etc.

   ☐ B   redefine range X only

   ☐ C   carry out all the processes of defining and enhancing and rename the graph

   ☐ D   do nothing

3. When you have named a graph, in order to use the named graph again at some future session, you should

   ☐ A   save the whole worksheet with /FS

   ☐ B   save the graph to a PIC file

   ☐ C   do nothing

   ☐ D   press /GNS (Graph, Name, Save)

4. You have named a series of different graphs. To select a particular named graph for viewing, you press

   ☐ A   /GNC

   ☐ B   /GNU

   ☐ C   /GNV

   ☐ D   none of these

104

5. The number of data ranges which you can plot on a particular graph is

☐ A 4 (A-D)

☐ B 6 (A-F)

☐ C 8 (A-H)

☐ D 12 (A-L)

6. You are viewing a graph on your monitor. You want to select a different graph which you have created and named. To select it and view it, the keypresses, before you highlight it and press <Enter> are

☐ A <Enter><Enter><Enter>

☐ B <Enter><Name><Use>

☐ C <Esc><Enter><Use>

☐ D any of these

7. One of the following formulae is incomplete. It is

☐ A (A14*1.2)+1000

☐ B A14*1.2+1000

☐ C +A14*1.2+1000

☐ D +A14*1.2+(1000)

8. You wish to protect all the cells of your current worksheet. The keypresses are

☐ A /WGPE

☐ B /WGPE<Enter>

☐ C /RGPE

☐ D /RPE<Enter>

9. The formula to add the values in cells F7..F9 is

☐ A @SUM(F7..F9)

☐ B @SUM(F9..F7)

☐ C +F7+F8+F9

☐ D any of these

10. You have protected your worksheet with the correct global command, and now you want to alter one of the formulae. Before you re-protect the worksheet, you can disable the protection by the keypresses:

☐ A /RGPD

☐ B /WGPD<Enter>

☐ C /WGDP

☐ D /WGPD

SESSION 9
A Simple Database

1. Objectives

At the end of this session, you will be able to:

- ❏ appreciate what a database is
- ❏ understand the meaning of records and fields
- ❏ create a simple database input range
- ❏ use the *data, fill* command to list numbers
- ❏ enter labels, dates and currency
- ❏ sort the database in various ways
- ❏ use the primary and secondary sort commands
- ❏ search the database for particular groups of records
- ❏ extract records from the database
- ❏ use some statistical functions
- ❏ alter the database with *move, insert, delete*.

2. Introduction

In the first eight sessions, you have been concerned with worksheets which have primarily calculated various numeric results.

In this session, you will learn how a spreadsheet can manipulate data.

A *database* is a collection of information about sets of things. These sets can be, for example, collections of books, compact disks, stamp collections. In business, examples are lists of customers, stocks of raw materials and stocks of finished goods.

In this session, you will create a small database of the personnel employed by the CDPublications Company. You will learn how to sort the database, search it for particular groups of employees and extract information from it. You will also learn how to calculate such things as the average salary.

3. Description of the model

CDPublications Company (referred to hereafter as CDP) have 20 staff on the payroll. These staff are listed in Figure 9a.

Each ROW is known as a RECORD, and contains details concerning a single member of staff.

Each COLUMN is known as a FIELD, and contains one particular piece of information concerning each record. The field NAMES are in row 3 (A3..G3).

For example, the record for Uriah Heep is in row 10 (A10..G10), and cell D10 is in the DEPARTMENT field (column D) and shows that he works in the ACCOUNTS department.

4. Notes on the design of the model

At present the employees are listed in numerical order of staff number (column A). However, you will soon learn to list them in any order you want, e.g. alphabetically by surname (column B).

Twenty staff are listed (rows 4..23), but obviously the list could be added to. Details of how to do this are given in paragraph 10 below.

There are seven fields (columns A..G), and again these could be added to. For example other fields could contain home addresses, home telephone numbers, National Insurance numbers, date started with the company etc.

5. Notes on creating the worksheet

The following notes refer to figure 9a.

COLUMN-WIDTHS

Column-widths are best set individually. Position the cursor over each column separately before using /WCS

Column A:	8
Column B:	14
Column C:	12
Column D:	12
Column E:	10
Column F:	3
Column G:	9

Column A

STAFFNO   Label: left-aligned

The numbers in cells A4..A23 can be entered as follows:

Position the cursor over cell A4

Press | /DF . | (Data, Fill, <.>)

Move cursor to cell A23 (Try <PgDn> <↑>)

Press | <Enter> |

Figure 9a

	A	B	C	D	E	F	G
1	CDPublications Company: Staff Database						
2							
3	STAFFNO	SURNAME	FIRSTNAME	DEPARTMENT	DOB	SEX	SALARY
4	1	PICKWICK	SAMUEL	ADMIN	31-Dec-29	M	50000
5	2	SNODGRASS	AUGUSTUS	MARKETING	15-Jul-31	M	18000
6	3	TUPMAN	TRACY	MARKETING	16-Nov-32	M	18000
7	4	WINKLE	NATHANIEL	MARKETING	05-Apr-35	M	18000
8	5	BARDELL	MARTHA	ACCOUNTS	22-Aug-38	F	17000
9	6	COPPERFIELD	DAVID	SALES	24-Dec-69	M	12000
10	7	HEEP	URIAH	ACCOUNTS	04-Sep-52	M	16000
11	8	MICAWBER	WILKINS	SALES	29-Jul-40	M	9000
12	9	TROTWOOD	BETSEY	PERSONNEL	28-Feb-28	F	11000
13	10	TWIST	OLIVER	ADMIN	02-Sep-72	M	4000
14	11	DEDLOCK	LEICESTER	ADMIN	19-May-30	M	35000
15	12	CRATCHIT	ROBERT	ACCOUNTS	14-Mar-51	M	5000
16	13	SCROOGE	EBENEZER	ACCOUNTS	30-Jan-34	M	22000
17	14	CRATCHIT	BELINDA	PERSONNEL	02-Apr-69	F	12000
18	15	DEDLOCK	VOLUMNIA	PERSONNEL	02-Dec-71	F	20000
19	16	DEDLOCK	HONORIA	MARKETING	23-Jun-37	F	25000
20	17	SQUEERS	WACKFORD	SECURITY	01-Jul-50	M	7500
21	18	BUZFUZ	SERGEANT	SECURITY	30-May-52	M	7500
22	19	SQUEERS	FANNY	PERSONNEL	07-Oct-53	F	8000
23	20	JINGLE	ALFRED	SALES	20-Nov-48	M	19000

Type | 1 <Enter> | against *Start* prompt

Type | <Enter> | against *Step*: 1 prompt

Type {**notAEA**} | <Enter> | against *Stop: 8191* prompt

[The programs vary slightly in the prompt words and numbers]

The cells A4..A23 should be filled with numbers 1..20

Columns B, C, D and F

All cells are labels, left-aligned

109

Column E

Cell E3: Label, centred. Press ┌─────────────────┐ `^DOB<Enter>` └─────────────────┘

Cells E4..E23: Do NOT enter the dates as shown. Use the following method to enter with the @DATE formula.

Move the cursor to cell E4

Type ┌──────────────────────────────┐ `@DATE(29,12,31)<Enter>` └──────────────────────────────┘

You will see the formula in the control panel and the number 10958 in the cell.

After @DATE, the figures entered in the brackets are (year,month,day), i e.:

(1)   the last two digits of the year: 29 of 1929

[The programs start counting from the beginning of the 20th century. {123}{VP} 21st century: the year 2099 will be entered as 199. {VP} starts with 1801 as -99.]

(2)   the month: Jan..Dec = 1..12

(3)   the day of the month: 1..31 or 1..30 or 1..28 or 1..29, depending on the month

The number appearing in the cell, e.g. 10958 is the number of days since the 1st January, 1900. This is useful for the program to use in sort calculations. However, to see the date in the cell in a more usual format,

Move the cursor to cell E4

Press ┌──────────────────┐ `/RFD` └──────────────────┘ (Range, Format, Date)

Choose a suitable format from the menu, e.g.

{123} DD-MMM-YY {AEA} D-M-Y or {VP} D-MMM-Y and press <Enter>

Move the cursor to E23 to define the range and press <Enter>

The cells E4..E23 should now show the dates in the format shown in figure 9a, the formulae (in the control panel) should be as entered, and the program will remember the number of days since 1st January, 1900.

Now move to cell E5

Press ┌──────────────────────────────┐ `@DATE(31,7,15)<Enter>` └──────────────────────────────┘

and so on for cells E6..E23.

Column G

Cell G3: Label, right-aligned. Press ┌──────────────────┐ `"SALARY` └──────────────────┘ <Enter>

Use /RFC0<Enter>[range]<Enter>

(Range, Format, Currency, 0) for the range G4..G23

110

Enter the salary figures from figure 9a into cells G4..G23, remembering that £50,000 must be entered as 50000

6. Sorting the database

Move the cursor to cell A4

Press | /DS | (Data, Sort)

These are the entry keys to data-sorting.

Press | D | (Data-Range)

Highlight the range A4..G23 and press <Enter>

Note that you did not include row 3, since the field names are not included in the sort.

Press | P | (Primary-Key)

You are going to sort the staff into alphabetical order, by Surname

Move the cursor to the SURNAME column. Any cell in the range B4..B23 will do.

Press | <Enter>A | (Ascending)

Pressing A for Ascending means that the names will be sorted in the order A..Z. Pressing D for Descending would sort the names in the order Z..A

Press | <Enter> |

You are returned to the *Sort* menu.

Press | G | (Go)

and the surnames are sorted A..Z, with Martha Bardell heading the list.

You will notice that the Dedlocks are together, but not necessarily in the order of their Firstnames. To correct this, you must also specify a Secondary-Key sort.

Press | /DSS | (Data, Sort, Secondary-Key)

Move the cursor to the *Firstname* field (range C4..C23)

Press | <Enter>A<Enter>G | (Ascending, Go)

and the Dedlocks should be in the order Honoria, Leicester, Volumnia.

Now try sorting the staff by date of birth, youngest first.

Press | /DSP |

Move the cursor to column E (press <Esc> if necessary first) and press <Enter>

Press | D<Enter>G |

111

Note that D for Descending was required, since the highest date-numbers are listed first.

Note that the Data-Range has already been set, and need only be changed if required before a fresh data-sort.

Next, try sorting the staff into departments, with the departments in alphabetical order, and, within the departments, the staff sorted in salary order, highest salaries first.

Press ┃ /DSP[rangeD4..D23]A<Enter>S[rangeG4..G23]D<Enter>G ┃

Ebenezer Scrooge should head the list with the highest salary in the accounts department.

Incidentally, you could freeze the first three rows so that you can keep the headings visible when you scroll to row 23.

> Move the cursor to row three, and press /WTH {AEA} /WBH

Now move the cursor to row 23 to see the security staff.

Feel free to carry out further primary and secondary sorts, until you are familiar with the procedure.

Finish up with re-sorting the database into the original order of staff numbers.

Press ┃ /DSP[rangeA4..A23]A<Enter>G<Home> ┃

7. Searching the database

Move the cursor to cell A4 if it is not already there.

{123}{VP}   Press ┃ /C<↑><Esc><↑>. ┃ (do not forget the full stop!)

{AEA}   Press ┃ /WBC ┃ move cursor to A3 and press ┃ /C. ┃

The cursor should now be on cell A3

> Move the cursor to cell G3, and press <Enter>

> Move the cursor to cell A30, and press <Enter>

Unless you have made a mistake, you should have copied the field names to cells A30..G30.

Cells A30..G30 are the first row of your criteria range.

> Enter F in cell F31, i.e in the cell below *SEX*

> {AEA} Enter * in cell A31

The F is the criteria for your search, and the criteria range is now A30..G31.

Press ┃ /DQC ┃ (Data, Query, Criterion)

> Highlight the criterion range A30..G31 and press <Enter>

You are taken back to the Query menu

112

Press ☐ I ☐ (Input)

Highlight the Input range A3..G23 and press **<Enter>**

Note particularly that, unlike as in sorting, you have now *included* the field names in the input range.

{AEA} At this stage, you should define the OutRange (as well as the Criteria and InpRange, which you have just done). AEA works differently from 1-2-3, though the principles are the same. When you come to Extracting Records in the next paragraph, you will not need to define OutRange again. Copy A30..G30 to A40..G40. Press **/DQO** (Data, Question, OutRange). Highlight A40..G40 and press **<Enter>**.

Press ☐ F ☐ (Find)

{123}{VP} Row 8 should be highlighted for you, since Martha Bardell is the first female on the staff list. Press **< ↓ >** and Betsey Trotwood is highlighted. Keep pressing **< ↓ >** until the last female staff member is highlighted. [You will hear a beep when the last item of the Find is reached.]

{AEA} Menu-like cards appear, one for each record which contains an F under SEX. Martha Bardell appears first. Keep pressing **<PgDn>** to view all the female staff. [You will hear a beep when the last item of Find is reached.]

Press {123} **<Esc>Q** {VP} **<Esc>** {AEA} **Q** to get back to READY mode.

Move the cursor to cell F31

Delete the *F* with **/RE<Enter>**

Now to find all staff whose salaries are in the range £10,000 and £20,000.

Enter the following formula in cell G31:

+G4>=10000#and#+G4<=20000

What this formula says is this:

Is the salary of Samuel Pickwick (his salary is in cell G4) greater than or equal to £10,000, AND ALSO is his salary less than or equal to £20,000? If so indicate this with a figure 1 (true), but if it is not true, indicate this with a figure 0 (false). Since S. Pickwick's salary is over £10,000 but is NOT also less than or equal to £20,000, then the answer is no, and you will see a figure 0 (false) in cell G31.

Note that the *logical operator* #AND# has a # at the beginning and end of AND.

Press ☐ /DQF ☐ (Data, Query, Find) and the down arrow ({AEA} **<PgDn>**) to find all the staff within the specified salary range.

Return to *READY* mode.

Do NOT delete the formula in cell G31.

113

Now enter the following formula in cell E31:

+E4>=@DATE(40,1,1)

Press | /DQF | to find all staff born on or after 1st January, 1940 whose salaries are £10,000 or more, but £20,000 or less. There are only five of them.

Return to *READY* mode.

Delete cells E31 and G31 with /RE

Enter SALES in cell D31 and ACCOUNTS in cell D32.

{AEA} Enter * in cell A32 as well.

Press | /DQC | (Data, Query, Criterion)

Press | <↓> | to highlight the range A30..G32.

[The criterion range must contain all the criteria cells, but must not contain any blank rows; this principle applies to the Input range as well.]

Press | <Enter> /DQF | to find all staff in the Sales and Accounts departments.

You should now be able to experiment with other searches of your own choice. For example, you could search for all staff whose surnames begin with the letter D. To do this, enter D* in cell B31. ({AEA} Do not forget the * in cell A31.) The * is known as a *wildcard* which means *all characters to the end of the label*. You must also reduce the criterion range to include only rows 30 and 31, since a blank row in the criteria range results in all records being selected. Use /RE to erase previous criteria no longer needed.

[There are many other facilities available for searching; for further details refer to the manual for your particular program.]

8. Extracting records

You may need to extract selected records from the database, show them elsewhere on the spreadsheet so that they can be viewed separately and, if required, printed out.

Suppose the Chairman is disturbed by discontent among the lower-paid staff. He wants a list of all staff whose salaries are £10,000 or less.

Delete any entries in your criteria range (rows 31 and below)

Enter the following formula in cell G31

+G4<=10000

{AEA} Also enter * in cell A31

{123}{VP} Copy the range A3..G3 to row A40..G40

114

{AEA} You have already done this. Check!

Press ╎   /DQC   ╎ (Data, Query, Criterion)

Specify the range A30..G31

Press ╎   O   ╎ (Output)

The control panel shows: *Enter Output Range*

Specify the range A40..G49

[This range gives 9 rows for the extracted output, which should be adequate. If you do not specify an adequate range, you would have to enlarge the range when you get an error message. If you specify the range A40..G40, i.e. a single line only, the program will use as many rows as necessary, but may erase data below them. You are going to use rows 50..55 in the next paragraph.]

Press ╎   E   ╎ (Extract)

Return to *READY* mode

View the extracted output in the range A40..G46

Micawber, Twist, Cratchit, W. Squeers, Buzfuz and F. Squeers should be listed.

You will note that they are listed in Staff Number order.

If the Chairman had wanted them listed in alphabetical order or in order of their salaries, you could have sorted the database appropriately before extracting the records.

Note that the Output range need not contain all the fields, and also the order of the output range need not be the field order of the database. To test this out, delete cells A41..G46, delete cell F40, alter cell B40 to read *FIRSTNAME* and cell C40 to read *SURNAME*. Press **/DQE** to view the revised extracted output. [You may have to reformat dates, widen columns, move headings together, depending on your program. Experiment!]

When you have finished experimenting, change A40..G40 back to its original form, i.e a copy of A30..G30, and reset column-widths, and delete output in rows 41 and below.

9. Database statistical functions

IF YOU ARE USING 1-2-3 OR VP

({AEA} see special section at the end of this paragraph.)

The database can be used to calculate, for example, the average salaries of the staff in the marketing and sales departments. To do so, you will use some of the database statistical functions.

In doing so, you will also learn about named ranges.

Move the cursor to cell A3

Press | /RNC | (Range, Name, Create)

Type | INPUT | (you can type in lowercase)

Press | <Enter> |

Specify the range A3..G23 and press **<Enter>**

Move the cursor to cell G31 and delete the formula there with **/RE<Enter>** or any other criteria you may have entered during your experiments.

Enter **MARKETING** in cell D31, and **SALES** in cell D32

Move the cursor to cell A30

Press | /RNC | (Range, Name, Create)

Type | CRITERIA | Press | <Enter> |

Specify the range A30..G32 and press **<Enter>**

You have now created two named ranges, and you will use these names in the formulae which follow below.

Enter the following labels in the appropriate cells:

A50:	**Marketing and Sales Staff:-**
B51:	**Average salary of staff**
B52:	**Highest paid staff member**
B53:	**Lowest paid staff member**
B54:	**Total staff salaries**
B55:	**Total number of staff**

Now enter the following formula in cell E51:

@DAVG($INPUT,6,$CRITERIA)

You should see the figure 17000 in cell E51. This is the average salary of all staff in marketing and sales.

Explanation:

The *@DAVG* is the formula for calculating the average salary of the salaries in column 6 (counting from the left, with column A being numbered 0), within the overall input range, and according to the criteria in the criteria range (marketing and sales). The formula is usually described as:

@DAVG(input,offset,criterion)

The dollar ($) signs are useful in this instance, because you are going to copy the formula to cells E52..E55. Without the dollar signs, the copied formulae would be relative, and would alter the input and criteria ranges. By copying the formula as it stands in cell E51, you can then edit the bits you want to change, thereby saving typing time.

116

Move the cursor to cell E51

Press `/C<Enter><↓>.<↓><↓><↓><Enter>`

This copies the formula in cell E51 to cells E52..E55

Now edit <F2> the copied formulae to read:

(The letters to replace AVG with are printed in BOLD, and note that you can enter the letters in lowercase.)

E52:	@**DMAX**($INPUT,6,$CRITERIA)
E53:	@**DMIN**($INPUT,6,$CRITERIA)
E54:	@**DSUM**($INPUT,6,$CRITERIA)
E55:	@**DCOUNT**($INPUT,6,$CRITERIA)

The results of the calculations should appear in the respective cells, i.e.:

E52: 25000; E53: 9000; E54: 119000; E55: 7

You could add £s and commas to E51..E54 with:

Move to cell E51

Press `/RFC0<Enter><↓><↓><↓><Enter>`

IF YOU ARE USING AEA [also of interest to users of {123} {VP}]

The database can be used to calculate, for example, the average salaries of the staff in the marketing and sales departments. To do so, you will use some of the statistical functions.

Move the cursor to cell G31 and delete the formula there with /RE<Enter> (and any other criteria you may have entered while experimenting).

Enter **MARKETING** in cell D31, and **SALES** in cell D32

Enter an * in each of cells A31 and A32.

Press /DQE to list Marketing and Sales staff in the output range A41..G47.

Enter the following labels in the appropriate cells:

A50:	**Marketing and Sales Staff:-**
B51:	**Average salary of staff**
B52:	**Highest paid staff member**
B53:	**Lowest paid staff member**
B54:	**Total staff salaries**
B55:	**Total number of staff**

Now enter the following formula in cell E51:

@AVG(G$41..G$47)

You should see the figure 17000 in cell E51. This is the average salary of all staff in marketing and sales.

Explanation:

The @AVG is the formula for calculating the average salary of the salaries in the range specified.

The dollar ($) signs are useful in this instance, because you are going to copy the formula to cells E52..E55. Without the dollar signs, the copied formulae would be relative. By copying the formula as it stands in cell E51, you can then edit the bits you want to change, thereby saving typing time.

> Move the cursor to cell E51
>
> Press `/C<Enter><↓>.<↓><↓><↓><Enter>`

This copies the formula in cell E51 to cells E52..E55

> Now edit <F2> the copied formulae to read:

(The letters to replace AVG with are printed in BOLD below. Note that you can enter the letters in lowercase.)

> E52: **@MAX**(G$41..G$47)
>
> E53: **@MIN**(G$41..G$47)
>
> E54: **@SUM**(G$41..G$47)
>
> E55: **@COUNT**(G$41..G$47)

The results of the calculations should appear in the respective cells, i.e.:

> E52: 25000; E53: 9000; E54: 119000; E55: 7

Note: instead of entering the range as G$41..G$47 you could first name the range using /RNC (Range, Name, Create), give it the name MARSAL (for example) and then use the name in the formula: @AVG(MARSAL). Use <F2> to edit cell E51 to try it.

You could now add £s and commas to E51..E54 with:

> Move to cell E51
>
> Press `/RFC0<Enter><↓><↓><↓><Enter>`

10. Altering the database

Before you end this session, you may like to learn how to move ranges and insert rows and columns.

> First, sort the database (A4..G23) into alphabetical order:
>
> Type `/DSP` (Data, Sort, Primary-Key)
>
> Move the cursor to column B, press <Enter>A<Enter>G

Nicholas Nickleby has joined the admin. staff as staff no. 21, and you wish to enter him into the database.

Move the cursor to cell A15

Type ⌶ /WIR<Enter> ⌶ (Worksheet, Insert, Row)

Mr. Pickwick moves down to make room for Nicholas, and you can now enter Nicholas's details. You can decide details such as his salary.

You will have to format the date (/RFD) and salary(/RFC0).

[If you want to delete a row, use /WDR (Worksheet, Delete, Row).]

Suppose you want to move the range A51..E56 to somewhere else on the worksheet, to leave more room for the output range above it. [Note that inserting Nicholas Nickleby has moved all the rows below him down a row.]

Move the cursor to cell A51

Type ⌶ /M ⌶ (Move)

Highlight the range A51..E56 and press <Enter>

Move the cursor to cell I51 and press <Enter>

Suppose now you wish to move column M to the right, to improve the layout if you want to print the statistics out.

Move the cursor to column M (say cell M52)

Type ⌶ /WIC<Enter> ⌶

To move it back again, make sure the cursor is in column M

Type ⌶ /WDC<Enter> ⌶

If you wish to practise moving, inserting and deleting, arrange the worksheet as you want it, save it with /FS<Enter>R, and then experiment as much as you wish before you quit this session (without saving any mess you have made!).

11. Summary

In this session you should have achieved the objectives set out at the start of this session.

In particular, you should have become acquainted with:

/DF	Data, Fill
@DATE	@Date(Year,Month,Day)
/RFD	Range, Format, Date
/RFC	Range, Format, Currency

119

/DSD	Data, Sort, Data-Range
/DSP	Data, Sort, Primary-key
/DSS	Data, Sort, Secondary-key
/DSG	Data, Sort, Go
/DQI	Data, Query, Input
/DQC	Data, Query, Criterion
/DQO	Data, Query, Output
/DQF	Data, Query, Find
/DQE	Data, Query, Extract
/RNC	Range, Name, Create
@AVG	Average(List) calculates average of values in the list
@MAX	Maximum(List) determines maximum value in the list
@MIN	Minimum(List) determines minimum value in the list
@SUM	Sum(Range) sums a range of cells
@COUNT	Count(List) counts the number of cells in the list

{123} {VP}:-

@DAVG	@DAVG(Input,Offset,Criterion) calculates the average of values in the offset column of the input range which meet the criteria of the criterion range.
@DMAX	@DMAX(Input,Offset,Criterion) indicates the maximum value in the offset column of the input range which meets the criteria of the criterion range.
@DMIN	@DMIN(Input,Offset,Criterion) indicates the minimum value in the offset column of the input range which meets the criteria of the criterion range.

120

```
@DSUM
```

@DSUM(Input,Offset,Criterion) adds the values in the offset column of the input range which meet the criteria of the criterion range.

```
@DCOUNT
```

@DCOUNT(Input,Offset,Criterion) counts the (non-blank) cells in the offset column of the input range which meet the criteria of the criterion range.

12. Activity

Look up the Share Prices page of a suitable newspaper, and choose a block of about 20 shares. Create a database using a choice of the column-headings (e.g. High, Low, Stock, Price, Yield, Index Code) as fields. Sort, find and extract records. Use statistical formulae to calculate any interesting statistics. Print out the database (total input range) and also any statistics you have identified, and any output you have extracted, with suitable title and headings.

13. Objective test ☐ A ☐ B ☑ C ☐ D

1. In a database, the vertical cells contain

   ☐ A records

   ☐ B fields

   ☐ C criteria

   ☐ D outputs

2. To fill a column with the figures 1,2,3,4,5,6,7,8,9,10, the quickest way is to use the command

   ☐ A /DF

   ☐ B /WDF

   ☐ C /RDF

   ☐ D /RFD

3. To enter the date 25th December 1991 in a database cell, the following entry shoud be made

   ☐ A '@DATE(91,12,25)

   ☐ B @DATE(25,12,91)

   ☐ C @DATE(91,12,25)

   ☐ D 25-Dec-91

4. To sort a list of surnames in column B into alphabetical order, where <→B> means "move the cursor to column B", and assuming the Data-range has already been defined, the keypresses are

   ☐ A /DS<→B>P<Enter>A<Enter>G

   ☐ B /DSP<→B><Enter>D<Enter>G

   ☐ C /DS<→B>P<Enter>D<Enter>G

   ☐ D /DSP<→B><Enter>A<Enter>G

5. When finding or extracting records, the criteria range can be defined by starting with the following keypresses:

   ☐ A /DC

   ☐ B /DQI

   ☐ C /DQC

   ☐ D /DI

6. The formula to find staff in the salary range £5,000 to £15,000 inclusive could be

   ☐ A +G4>=5000#AND#+G4<=15000

   ☐ B +G4<=5000#AND#+G4>=15000

   ☐ C +G4>=15000#AND#+G4<=5000

   ☐ D +G4>=£5,000#AND#+G4<=£15,000

7. Before extracting records, it is necessary to have defined one of the following:

   ☐ A the input range

   ☐ B the output range

   ☐ C the criterion range

   ☐ D all of these

8. To name a range with the name FRED, the keypresses before defining the range are

   ☐ A /WNCFRED

   ☐ B /RNCFRED

   ☐ C /RNC<Enter>FRED

   ☐ D /UNCLEFRED

9. The keypresses to insert a row in a worksheet, after positioning the cursor over the place where you want the row inserted, are

    ☐ A /RIR

    ☐ B /RIC

    ☐ C /WIR

    ☐ D /WRC

10. One of the following statements is true; the others are false. The true statement is

    ☐ A database fields can contain labels and values

    ☐ B data sorts require the field names in the data-range

    ☐ C query finds require the field names in the input range

    ☐ D +E4>=@DATE(40.1.1) is a legitimate formula

SESSION 10
Simple Macros

1. Objectives

At the end of this session, you will be able to:

- ❑ appreciate what a macro is
- ❑ create simple keyboard macros to
    - ❑ add £s and commas to values
    - ❑ return currency format to general format
    - ❑ set a column-width to 20
    - ❑ insert rows
- ❑ create a pro-forma table for interest factors
- ❑ create a macro to form a table of present values (DCF)

and, if you complete the Activity:

- ❑ create macros to form tables for:
    - ❑ present values (annuities)
    - ❑ future values (compound interest)
    - ❑ future values (annuities)

2. Introduction

In this session, you will be introduced to macros. These are, in their simplest form, a means of automating a succession of keystrokes. In their most advanced form they provide a language of immense programming capabilities. We are not concerned in this session with the latter. However, by the end of this session you will be able to create simple macros which will automate your most frequently used keystroke sequences. In addition, to finish this session, you will construct a table from which, with simple macros, you can read future or present values.

Follow the instructions carefully, step by step. In doing so, you will start to learn how to construct macros, and perhaps begin to realise their potential.

3. A simple macro

You will need some material on which to practise your macros.

Retrieve your *ZEDGRAPH* worksheet which you saved in session 7 (paragraphs 8 and 12). This should appear on your monitor as range A1..F13 of figure 10a.

Figure 10a

	A	B	C	D	E	F
1			The Zed Bicycle Company			
2			Budgeted Sales for Next Year			
3						
4	Qtr:-	Spring	Summer	Autumn	Winter	Totals
5	-------	-------	-------	-------	-------	-------
6	Model:-	£	£	£	£	£
7	Alpha	80,000	96,000	115,200	138,240	429,440
8	Beta	90,000	99,000	108,900	119,790	417,690
9	Gamma	80,000	80,000	90,000	90,000	340,000
10	Delta	60,000	54,000	58,600	52,740	225,340
11	-------	-------	-------	-------	-------	-------
12	Totals	310,000	329,000	372,700	400,770	1,412,470
13	=======	=======	=======	=======	=======	=======
14						
15	\c	/wg	invokes the Worksheet Global command			
16		f	invokes the Format command			
17		c	invokes Currency, to add £s and commas to values			
18		0	chooses O (zero) to give no decimal places			
19		~	imitates the <Enter> key			
20						
21	\x	/wg	invokes the Worksheet Global command			
22		f	invokes the Format command			
23		g	General, returns Format to original condition			
24						
25	\t	/wcs	invokes Worksheet Column Set-Width			
26		20~	sets column-width at 20			
27						
28	\i	/wi	invokes Worksheet Insert			
29		r	invokes Row			
30		{down}{down}	moves cursor down to insert THREE rows			
31		~	imitates the <Enter> key			

You will see on figure 10a some strange entries below this range. These are macros, and you are about to create the first one.

> Move the cursor to cell A15

> Type [`'\c`] Press [<Enter>]

This entry is purely for reference purposes, as will be explained later. Note that it is important to enter it as a label, i.e. with a label prefix ('); otherwise the cell will fill with the letter c. This principle applies to other entries which follow.

> Move to cell B15

> Type [`'/wg`] Press [<Enter>]

This is the first line of the macro, and contains the instruction "press the / key, followed by the w key and then the g key".

The objective of this macro is to change all values in the worksheet from plain format (e.g. 80000) to currency format (e.g. £80,000). The full set of keystrokes is /WGFC0<Enter> (Worksheet, Global, Format, Currency, 0 (zero), <Enter>). When you have completed the macro, all you will have to do is press <Alt>+<c> and your macro will perform the keystrokes /WGFC0<Enter> for you.

You could enter the whole macro in cell B15. The disadvantage of this is that with longer and more complex macros, it would be difficult to understand it and detect any errors; also you might forget what it was meant to achieve. It is therefore customary to split the macro down into shorter pieces, with an explanation of each stage to the right of the commands.

Move the cursor to cell C15

Type | invokes the Worksheet Global command |

This is the explanation of the entries in cell B15, and is not part of the macro itself. The macro is listed in column B, starting in cell B15, and continuing down column B as far as is necessary. The macro stops when it encounters a blank line, in this case cell B20, if you refer to figure 10a.

Now enter the rest of the macro itself:

Cell B16:   Type **f**

Cell B17:   Type **c**

Cell B18:   Type **'0** (a zero, as a label)

Cell B19:   Type **~** (a tilde, which is the squiggly line sign, like an inverted S on its side, on some keyboards placed over the # sign, i.e. <Shift>+<#>). This tilde sign has the same effect as pressing <Enter>.

Now enter the explanations into cells C16..C19:

C16: Type **invokes the Format command**

C17: Type **invokes Currency, to add £s and commas to values**

C18: Type **chooses 0 (zero) to give no decimal places**

C19: Type **imitates the <Enter> key**

The final stage before trying it out is to NAME the macro.

Move the cursor to the first line of the macro itself, i.e. cell B15, and

Press | /RNC | (Range, Name, Create)

Against the prompt *Enter name*

Type | \c | Press | <Enter> |

126

Press [<Enter>] again to accept the range B15..B15

The macro is now named \C which is the equivalent of <Alt>+<c>

[You can use any letter of the alphabet: total 26.]

Now the try out your macro.

Press [<Alt>+<C>]

and all the values in the worksheet should change to the currency format, unless you have made a mistake somewhere.

4. Three more macros

If you refer to figure 10a, you will see three more macros, in the same format as the one you have just created.

Using the same principles for entry as for the \c macro, enter these into your worksheet.

Here are some notes to help you:

Do not forget to enter all cells as labels; this is very easy to forget, so go slowly!

Do not forget to NAME (/RNC) the macro in the top cell in column B with the name which is entered in column A to help you remember.

You must leave a blank row between each macro; otherwise each macro will execute in turn once you activate the top one.

Warning: Save your worksheet frequently to disk, particularly before trying out a new macro. If the macro misbehaves, you could lose a lot of your work, but if you have saved to disk, you can always retrieve the most recently saved version of your worksheet. You have been warned.

\x This macro changes all the values in the worksheet back to the original plain format, e.g. £80,000 back to 80000.

\t This macro sets the column-width at 20 for the column on which the cursor is placed when the macro is invoked. This macro is useful for widening column A to enter labels, e.g. for a Profit & Loss Account.

\i Note the entry {down}{down} in cell B30. The keyword {down} is a special key representing the cursor key movement of <↓> or down-arrow. [Other examples are {up} {right} {left} {home} {end} {pgup} {pgdn}. Note the curly-brackets which are essential.]

{AEA} uses {dn} for {down} {rt} for {right} {lt} for {left}

See manual for full details.

127

Before trying out this macro, move the cell pointer to row 11 (over the dotted lines). Press <Alt>+<i>, and three blank rows appear for rows 11, 12 and 13; useful if you want to enter three more models of bicycle (? the Epsilon, Zeta and Eta).

These are four simple macros to introduce you to the idea. If you want to create some more for successive keystrokes which you use often, you can construct them using the principles which you have learned so far. You will need to refer to the manual for your particular program to advance further.

5. Moving the macros

So far you have placed the macros below the worksheet. This was done so that you could see the macros and worksheet easily. However, this was not a very good idea, because if you make changes to the worksheet itself, these changes (e.g. inserting columns and rows) could upset the macros. So it is customary to place the macros well away from the likely total working area. Try this:

Move the macros to cell GG999:

> Move the cursor to cell A15

Press `     /M     ` (Move)

Highlight the range A15..C31. Press <Enter>

Type `   GG999   ` Press `   <Enter>   `

To find the macros, press <End> <Home>

To return to the worksheet table, press <Home>

The macros should still work. Try them!

6. Using the macros again

If you think you may want to use the four macros you have just created in a new worksheet, try this:

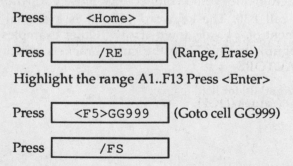

`/FS<Enter>R` (File, Save, Replace)

This saves *ZEDGRAPH* in its current form.

Press `   <Home>   `

Press `    /RE    ` (Range, Erase)

Highlight the range A1..F13 Press <Enter>

Press `  <F5>GG999  ` (Goto cell GG999)

Press `    /FS    `

Type | MACROS | Press | <Enter>

This creates a new file called *MACROS*.

The next time you want to create a new worksheet containing your macros, retrieve *MACROS* and you will start at cell GG999, which reminds you that your macros are there. [You can at this stage erase any that you will not want to use.] Then press <Home> to get to the blank cells at the top left-hand corner of the spreadsheet. When you save your new worksheet (which should be soon!), save it with a new filename. You can then use your *MACROS* file as often as you need it.

In fact, you are now in the worksheet called *MACROS*.

To get back to your *ZEDGRAPH* worksheet,

Press | /FR | (File, Retrieve)

Highlight *ZEDGRAPH* and press **<Enter>**

7. A table of present value factors: Introduction

Now for a rather more ambitious project. You are going to create a *Present Value* or *Discounted Cash Flow (DCF)* table. If you want to see what one looks like, you can sometimes find one at the end of finance or management accounting text-books which cover the subject of Project Appraisal or Capital Budgeting. For example, AFBIS has one in the Appendix, where it is called *TABLE 1 - PRESENT VALUE FACTORS*. You do not need to understand the subject to construct this table; simply follow the instructions. However, if you want to have some idea of how the table can be used in business, you can find an explanation in AFBIS, section on *Project Appraisal*, or in any other appropriate text-book or manual.

The table you will construct will calculate present values automatically, by pressing <Alt>+<A>. If you want to expand the table in size, to make it more comprehensive, and to make it do other clever things, such as calculate future values and annuities, then you are referred to ACTIVITY paragraph 11 towards the end of this session. Guidance is given there on how to do this.

8. Creating the PV table

Start with a blank spreadsheet; do NOT start with the *MACROS* spreadsheet which you created in paragraph 6 because the macro names could conflict with those you will make here.

Make the following entries:- [You can check them against Figure 10b]

Cell A1:   **TABLE OF INTEREST FACTORS**
Cell A2:   \- and copy A2 to B2..H2
Cell A3:   **Press <Alt>+A for Present Values (DCF)**
Cell A7:   \- and copy A7 to B7..H7
Cell A9   \- and copy A9 to B9..H9

129

Cell A10:   **PERIODS:**

Cell A11:   **0**   (a zero)

Cell A12:   **+A11+1**

[Note: Rows 4, 5 and 6 are left blank, so that additional macro instructions can be entered here if you carry out the activity in paragraph 11 below. Row 8 is left blank so that each macro, when activated, can enter a description here.]

Move the cursor to cell A12

Press │ `/C<Enter><↓>.` (a full stop) │

Move the cursor to cell A21, and press **<Enter>**

This copies the formula in cell A12 to cells A13..A21, and produces period numbers 0..10 in cells A11..A21.

Next you need interest rates in row 10.

You could, of course, enter all the rates from 1% to say 50% in stages of 1%, but this would create a very large worksheet which, at this stage in your learning process, would be rather inappropriate. Also large spreadsheets take longer to recalculate, unless you have a fast computer or maths co-processor chip. So for now, you will start at 5% and progress in 5% stages to 35%.

Enter in cell B10:   **.05**

Enter in cell C10:   **+B10+.05**

Copy cell C10 to cells D10..H10

[You should know how to do this by now!]

Move to cell B10

Press │ `/RFP0<Enter>` │ (Range, Format, Percent, zero)

Highlight the range B10..H10, and press **<Enter>**

This changes 0.05 to 5% in cell B10, and so on.

Next, to enter the macro itself. Make the following entries, being very careful to get them exactly right.

Cell A25:   **'\a**

This is for reference purposes only, and gives the name of the macro. Don't forget the ' to make it a label.

Cell B25:   **{goto}a8~Present Values of £1 at the end of n periods~**

This tells the cursor to go to cell A8, and enter the label which then appears in cell A8 to tell you what the table shows.

Cell B26:   **{goto}b11~1/((1+b$10)^$a11)~**

This tells the cursor to go to cell B11, and enter the present value formula, which is the reciprocal of the compound interest formula, i.e 1 divided by (=reciprocal): 1 plus the interest rate (which is the 5% in cell B10), to the power of the number of years (which is the 0 in cell A11). The caret sign (^) is usually <Shift>+<6> on the keyboard, and stands for "to the power of". The $ signs are purely to keep the following numbers absolute rather than relative when copying the formula into other cells, which the next line of the macro performs. Don't forget the tildes (~) after b11 and at the end of the formula. Another easy thing to forget is that all brackets must be complete pairs e.g. (( )); there are two pairs in the formula.

[An explanation of the formula is given in AFBIS, chapter entitled *Principles of Discounted Cash Flow*.]

Cell B27:   **'/cb11~b12.b21~**

Don't forget the ' to start with; otherwise your commands will be obeyed! And don't forget the tildes.

This tells the program to copy cell B11 to cells B12..B21

Cell B28:   **'/cb11.b21~c11.h21~**

This tells the program to copy cells B11..B21 to cells C11..H21.

Finally, NAME the macro.

> With the cursor on cell B25,

> Press | /RNC\a<Enter><Enter> |

9. Testing the PV table

Now for the moment of truth.

> Press | <Alt>+A |

How long the macro takes to work depends on the speed of your computer. Be patient. Row 8 should show the title, and cells B11..H21 should fill with figures. If this does not happen, or the figures look wrong, check that your entries in B25..B28 are correct. [When the author tried it, he had forgotten to enter one of the tildes.]

The figures in the table look rather untidy; they are shown to six decimal places (if the global column-width is set at 9). To make the figures show to three decimal places:

> Press | /WGFF3<Enter> | (Worksheet, Global, Format, Fixed, 3)

Column A (Periods) now looks untidy, showing the periods (years) to three decimal places; so

> Move the cursor to cell A11

> Press | /RFF0<Enter> | (Range, Format, Fixed, 0)

131

Move the cursor to cell A21, and press <Enter>

Note that the percentage figures in row 10 were not affected by the Global Format command, since Range commands take precedence over global commands.

Your worksheet should look like Figure 10b.

Figure 10b

	A	B	C	D	E	F	G	H
1	TABLE OF INTEREST FACTORS							
2	--							
3	Press <Alt>+A for Present Values (DCF)							
4								
5								
6								
7	--							
8	Present Values of £1 at the end of n periods							
9	--							
10	PERIODS:	5%	10%	15%	20%	25%	30%	35%
11	0	1.000	1.000	1.000	1.000	1.000	1.000	1.000
12	1	.952	.909	.870	.833	.800	.769	.741
13	2	.907	.826	.756	.694	.640	.592	.549
14	3	.864	.751	.658	.579	.512	.455	.406
15	4	.823	.683	.572	.482	.410	.350	.301
16	5	.784	.621	.497	.402	.328	.269	.223
17	6	.746	.564	.432	.335	.262	.207	.165
18	7	.711	.513	.376	.279	.210	.159	.122
19	8	.677	.467	.327	.233	.168	.123	.091
20	9	.645	.424	.284	.194	.134	.094	.067
21	10	.614	.386	.247	.162	.107	.073	.050
22								
23								
24								
25	\a	{goto}a8~Present Values of £1 at the end of n periods~						
26		{goto}b11~1/((1+b$10)^$a11						
27		/cb11~b12.b21~						
28		/cb11.b21~c11.h21~						

Save your present worksheet with the name *INTABS*, i.e a mnemonic for INTerest TABles.

If you want to continue now, or at some later time, with the activity in paragraph 11 below, please do!

Also you may want to get further practice with the three PRACTICE SESSIONS (11 - 13) which follow this session.

Otherwise, since this is the final main session, the author hopes you have (on the whole) enjoyed working through these sessions, and feel more confident about spreadsheets. No doubt you made many mistakes as you went along, but you learn by mistakes, however frustrated you may feel at the time. You have, of course, only scratched the surface of spreadsheet potential, but, on the other hand, you should have learnt enough to create some basic worksheets, graphs, databases and macros of your own.

Do not be afraid to experiment! Explore your manuals!

Enjoy yourself!

10. Summary

In this session you should have achieved the objectives set out at the start of this session.

In particular, you should have become acquainted with:

- planning a macro
- positioning a macro (out of the way)
- entering a macro:

    N.B.   all labels; one column only; no blank rows

- annotating a macro
- naming a macro (top cell of macro) /RNC\x

~	(a tilde) = <Enter>
^	(a caret) = to the power of
{down}	<↓> moves the cursor down a row
{up}	<↑> moves the cursor up a row
{right}	<→> moves the cursor one column right
{left}	<←> moves the cursor one column left
{goto}	<F5> GoTo

11. Activity

Recover your file INTABS which you saved at the end of paragraph 9.

Create three more macros for this worksheet, as follows:

Copy cells A25..B28 to A30..B33, then to A35..B39, and again to A40..B43. Since the four macros contain formulae with similar elements, you can edit each block of macro cells, rather than create them from scratch.

MACRO B

Cell A30: Edit the name to show \b

Title: **Present Values of £1 per period for n periods**

[Edit cell B30 to show this revised title.]

Formula: **@PV(1,b$10,$a11)**

[Edit cell B31 to show this revised formula.]

Note: the formula @PV(payments,interest,term) determines the present value of an investment.

The entries in the last two lines of the macro (B32 and B33) stay the same as for macro A. The same applies to macros C and D.

Cell A4 could contain:

Press <Alt>+B for Present Values (Annuities)

[Tip for macros C and D: The copy command can be used to copy formulae from one macro to another before editing. Look for similar formulae.]

MACRO C

Cell A5:	**Press <Alt>+C for Future Values**
Title:	**Future Values of £1 at the end of n periods**
Formula:	**((1+b$10)^$a11)**

MACRO D

Cell A6:	**Press <Alt>+D for Future Values (Annuities)**
Title:	**Future Values of £1 per period for n periods**
Formula:	**@fv(1,b$10,$a11)**

[Tip: Don't forget to NAME the macros.]

Now try out all four of your macros. Keep your fingers crossed!

If your macros do not work, check all your typing meticulously. In addition it may help if you annotate each row of the macro, in a column to the right (e.g. column I, which would not over-write the macros extending from column B). You were recommended to do so (and shown how) in the first part of this session, in the five macros for ZED Bicycle Company. The discipline of doing so usually identifies any error in the macro, such as a missing tilde, comma, bracket, $ sign.

If you feel really energetic, you could move the macros to a safe place on the spreadsheet, and expand the worksheet to show all percentages in stages of 1% from 1% to 50%, and increase the period (year) coverage from 10 to 25 years. Recalculation time when you activate the macro will depend on the speed of your computer.

12. Objective test ☐ A ☐ B ☑ C ☐ D

1. You have planned a macro which will carry out the procedure for naming any macro up to the stage of actually typing in the name, i.e. /RNC. You have decide to give this macro the unique name of N. As a memorandum, you type the name of this macro into cell A20, pressing

    ☐ A '\n

    ☐ B \'n

    ☐ C '/n

    ☐ D /'n

2. Next, you move to cell B20 to type in the macro. You press

    ☐ A   /rnc

    ☐ B   '/rnc

    ☐ C   '/rnc~

    ☐ D   '\rnc~

3. To test the macro at this stage, you press

    ☐ A   <Alt>+N

    ☐ B   <Ctrl>+N

    ☐ C   <Alt> N

    ☐ D   none of these

4. To name the macro you have created in Q2, (with the cursor on cell B20) you press

    ☐ A   /rnc\n<Enter><Enter>

    ☐ B   '/rnc\n<Enter>

    ☐ C   '\rnc/n<Enter><Enter>

    ☐ D   /rnc\n<Enter>

5. You wish to annotate this macro with "Invokes Range, Name, Create". A good place to enter this is in cell

    ☐ A   B21

    ☐ B   B19

    ☐ C   C20

    ☐ D   A20

6. The sign for <Enter> in a macro is

    ☐ A   ~ (a tilde)

    ☐ B   ^ (a caret)

    ☐ C   {~} (a tilde in curly braces)

    ☐ D   {^} (a caret in curly braces)

7. Only one of the following statements is true. It is

    ☐ A {Curly Braces} are optional for macro keywords

    ☐ B a ' must be typed before {curly braces} to make it a label

    ☐ C macros can be split over columns as an alternative to rows

    ☐ D {GOTO} is the macro keyword for <F5>

8. Only one of the following formulae is correct

    ☐ A 1/(1+B$10)^$A11)~

    ☐ B 1/((1+B$10)$^A11)~

    ☐ C 1/((1+B$10)^$A11~

    ☐ D 1/((1+B$10)^$A11)~

9. The figures for periods in column A of a table should be 1, 2, 3 etc. On the worksheet, due to having set a global format, they appear as 1.000, 2.000, 3.000 etc. To correct this for the range, the intitial keystrokes to correct this are

    ☐ A /RFC0<Enter>[range]<Enter>

    ☐ B /RFF.<Enter>[range]<Enter>

    ☐ C /RFF0<Enter>[range]<Enter>

    ☐ D none of these

10. You have planned and created a long and marvellous macro, but, when you try it out, it will not work properly. You have just spent all evening unsuccessfully trying to debug it. The best thing to do is to

    ☐ A try putting tildes at the end of every line

    ☐ B ring up a friend who knows about these things

    ☐ C import the file to a wordprocessor and use the spellchecker

    ☐ D go to bed, and sleep on it.

PRACTICE SESSION 11
Cost Behaviour

1. Introduction

In this session, and in practice sessions 12 and 13, you have an opportunity to attempt to solve some problems, using the skills you have acquired during the previous sessions. The problems are concerned with management accounting.

The problems can, of course, be solved with pencil and paper. However, they can be solved more efficiently on a spreadsheet. The formulae needed are fairly simple. If you get stuck, you can refer to the solution in paragraph 3, which refers you to two figures: the first showing the design of the worksheet, and the second the same worksheet printed out with the formulae used in the corresponding cells.

A suggested approach is:
- ❑ study the problem carefully
- ❑ revise the theory if you cannot recollect it properly
- ❑ plan the layout of the worksheet required for the solution
- ❑ enter the headings on the worksheet as labels
- ❑ fill in the values from the data
- ❑ adjust any column widths to make the worksheet more comfortable to work with
- ❑ enter the first formula required
- ❑ check the results of the formula against the correct figure (use a calculator if necessary)
- ❑ copy the formula to any cells which will benefit
- ❑ test-check the results of the copied formulae against the correct figures
- ❑ if necessary, correct the original formula (e.g. for $ signs)
- ❑ copy the formula again to the appropriate cells
- ❑ repeat the checking, correcting and copying procedure as often as necesary to achieve a satisfactory result
- ❑ enter the next formula, and repeat the previous procedure
- ❑ continue until you are satisfied that the results are satisfactory
- ❑ tidy up the worksheet with lines and general layout, using move and insert commands as necessary

    ❑ compare your results with the suggested solution in figures lla and llb

    ❑ congratulate yourself because yours is better.

2. The problem

A. AUCKLAND

Listed below are total costs at two different levels of activity for the business of Audrey Auckland. Audrey wants to know, for each item of cost, how much is variable and how much is fixed.

Prepare a table for her, showing the costs as shown in the data, and:

- variable costs per unit
- total variable costs at the lower activity level
- total variable costs at the higher activity level
- total fixed costs

Production/sales levels (units)	2,000	5,000
	Total costs	
	£	£
Supervision	20,000	20,000
Direct materials	100,000	250,000
Storage & handling	10,000	17,500
Maintenance	30,000	60,000
Direct wages	90,000	225,000
Eiectricity	10,000	19,000
Rent	26,000	26,000
Insurance	8,000	8,000
Salesmen's salaries (incl. commission)	50,000	65,000
Packaging	27,500	68,750
Staff salaries	80,000	80,000
Distribution	30,000	52,500
Rates	20,000	20,000
Depreciation	40,000	40,000

3 . The solution

Reference should be made to figures lla and llb.

An example of the calculations is for Electricity:

	Production/sales units	Cost £s
	5,000	19,000
less:	2,000	10,000
= change:	3,000	9,000

$$\frac{\text{Change in cost (£s)}}{\text{Change in units}} = \frac{£9,000}{3,000} = £3.00 \text{ per unit}$$

If you refer to the figures lla and llb, you will see that the formula in cell D16 reflects this:

(C16-B16)/ ($C$4-$B$4)

Costs which change with levels of activity are variable costs; therefore £3.00 is the variable cost per unit.

The total variable costs in cells E16 and F16 are obtained by multiplying the variable cost per unit (£3 in cell D16) by the number of units (2,000 in cell B4 and 5,000 in cell C4).

The total fixed costs cell G16 are obtained by subtracting the total variable costs in cell F16 from the total costs in cell C16. (Alternatively, the total fixed costs cell G16 could be obtained by subtracting the total variable costs in cell E16 from the total costs in cell B16.)

Comment: This can be a useful table for budgeting fixed costs.

For example, you could take the monthly profit and loss account expenditure figures for the past year, and find two months which had low and high levels of production/sales.

The figures could be entered into the table, and the total of column G would give an indication of the total fixed costs for a typical month. Multiply by 12 and adjust for anticipated inflation and any known changes in fixed costs to arrive at a budgeted figure for fixed costs for next year.

[This problem is an adaptation of an example from the chapter entitled *Cost Behaviour* in AFBIS, to which reference could be made for a more detailed explanation of the principles of cost behaviour.]

Figure 11a

	A	B	C	D	E	F	G
1	A. AUCKLAND						
2	Analysis of Fixed and Variable Costs						
3	---						
4	Production/Sales (units):-	2,000	5,000	1	2,000	5,000	Any
5	---						
6				Per Unit	Total	Total	Total
7		Total	Total	Variable	Var.	Var.	Fixed
8		Costs	Costs	Costs	Costs	Costs	Costs
9	Expenditure:	£	£	£	£	£	£
10	---						
11	Supervision	20,000	20,000	.00	0	0	20,000
12	Direct Materials	100,000	250,000	50.00	100,000	250,000	0
13	Storage & Handling	10,000	17,500	2.50	5,000	12,500	5,000
14	Maintenance	30,000	60,000	10.00	20,000	50,000	10,000
15	Direct Wages	90,000	225,000	45.00	90,000	225,000	0
16	Electricity	10,000	19,000	3.00	6,000	15,000	4,000
17	Rent	26,000	26,000	.00	0	0	26,000
18	Insurance	8,000	8,000	.00	0	0	8,000
19	Salesmen's Sals/Commission	50,000	65,000	5.00	10,000	25,000	40,000
20	Packaging	27,500	68,750	13.75	27,500	68,750	0
21	Staff Salaries	80,000	80,000	.00	0	0	80,000
22	Distribution	30,000	52,500	7.50	15,000	37,500	15,000
23	Rates	20,000	20,000	.00	0	0	20,000
24	Depreciation	40,000	40,000	.00	0	0	40,000
25	===						

Figure 11b

	A	B	C	D	E	F	G
1	A. Auckland						
2	Analysis of Fixed and Variable Cost						
3	---						
4	Production/Sales (units)	2,000	5,000	1	+B4	+C4	Any
5	---						
6				Per Unit	Total	Total	Total
7		Total	Total	Variable	Var.	Var.	Fixed
8		Costs	Costs	Costs	Costs	Costs	Costs
9	Expenditure:	£	£	£	£	£	£
10	---						
11	Supervision	20,000	20,000	(C11-B11)/($C$4-$B$4)	+$B$4*D11	+$C$4*D11	+C11-F11
12	Direct Materials	100,000	250,000	(C12-B12)/($C$4-$B$4)	+$B$4*D12	+$C$4*D12	+C12-F12
13	Storage & Handling	10,000	17,500	(C13-B13)/($C$4-$B$4)	+$B$4*D13	+$C$4*D13	+C13-F13
14	Maintenance	30,000	60,000	(C14-B14)/($C$4-$B$4)	+$B$4*D14	+$C$4*D14	+C14-F14
15	Direct Wages	90,000	225,000	(C15-B15)/($C$4-$B$4)	+$B$4*D15	+$C$4*D15	+C15-F15
16	Electricity	10,000	19,000	(C16-B16)/($C$4-$B$4)	+$B$4*D16	+$C$4*D16	+C16-F16
17	Rent	26,000	26,000	(C17-B17)/($C$4-$B$4)	+$B$4*D17	+$C$4*D17	+C17-F17
18	Insurance	8,000	8,000	(C18-B18)/($C$4-$B$4)	+$B$4*D18	+$C$4*D18	+C18-F18
19	Salesmen's Sals/Commissi	50,000	65,000	(C19-B19)/($C$4-$B$4)	+$B$4*D19	+$C$4*D19	+C19-F19
20	Packaging	27,500	68,750	(C20-B20)/($C$4-$B$4)	+$B$4*D20	+$C$4*D20	+C20-F20
21	Staff Salaries	80,000	80,000	(C21-B21)/($C$4-$B$4)	+$B$4*D21	+$C$4*D21	+C21-F21
22	Distribution	30,000	52,500	(C22-B22)/($C$4-$B$4)	+$B$4*D22	+$C$4*D22	+C22-F22
23	Rates	20,000	20,000	(C23-B23)/($C$4-$B$4)	+$B$4*D23	+$C$4*D23	+C23-F23
24	Depreciation	40,000	40,000	(C24-B24)/($C$4-$B$4)	+$B$4*D24	+$C$4*D24	+C24-F24
25	===						

PRACTICE SESSION 12
Overhead Cost Allocation and Apportionment

1. Introduction

In this session you will have an opportunity to solve another problem, using a spreadsheet as a vehicle for entering the data and displaying the solution.

If you have not already attempted practice session 11, please read its introduction before attempting this session. In any case, you may benefit from reading the suggested approach in that introduction again.

2. The problem

L. LORD

Lesley Lord operates a small business manufacturing cricket bats and tennis raquets. There are three production cost centres, namely machining, assembly and finishing departments. The overheads budget for next year is set out below, together with the cost centre details, and Lesley asks you for the annual cost of running each production cost centre.

Annual Overheads Budget:

	£
Rent	20,000
Rates	40,000
Consumables	10,000
Power	4,750
Cleaning	6,000
Light and heat	2,120
Maintenance	10,200
Depreciation – Machinery	8,000
Depreciation – Building	15,900
Indirect wages	19,600
Canteen	23,800
Insurance – Machinery	4,250
Insurance – Building	5,300
Supervision	42,000
Total	211,920

141

Cost Centre Details:

	Machining	Assembly	Finishing	Total
Area (square metres)	5,000	2,000	3,000	10,000
Volume (cubic metres)	25,000	10,000	18,000	53,000
Capital values (£000s)	70,000	10,000	5,000	85,000
Personnel (number)	10	20	5	35
Machinery (hp/hours)	8,750	350	400	9,500
Maintenance (£s)	9,500	500	200	10,200
Dep'n of machinery (£s)	6,500	1,000	500	8,000
Consumables (£s)	8,000	1,000	1,000	10,000

3. Suggested solution

Reference should be made to figures 12a and 12b.

The total overhead cost of each cost centre may be obtained by constructing an Overhead Cost Analysis Statement, sometimes referred to as an Overhead Cost Distribution Summary. This statement allocates costs to each cost centre if they are cost centre direct costs. If they are cost centre indirect costs, then they are apportioned or shared between the cost centres using a suitable basis of apportionment.

ALLOCATION

The items which have been marked (allocation) in figures 12a and 12b have been allocated to cost centres, since the overhead is directly attributable to those cost centres without apportionment being necessary.

Example: Consumables – the entry in cell D33 is +D17 which means that the figure of £8,000 is taken straight from cell D17 in the Data Entry Block.

APPORTIONMENT

All other items have been charged proportionately to cost centres using a suitable basis of apportionment.

Example: Rent has been apportioned using floor area occupied as a basis. Thus:

$$\text{Total cost to be apportioned} \times \frac{\text{Cost centre's share of basis}}{\text{Total apportionment basis}}$$

$$\text{Machining} = £20,000 \times \frac{5,000 \text{ square metres}}{10,000 \text{ square metres}}$$

Figure 12a

	A	B	C	D	E	F	G
1	L. LORD						
2	Overhead Cost Allocation and Apportionement						
3	==						
4	DATA ENTRY BLOCK						
5	--						
6	ANNUAL OVERHEADS BUDG	£	COST CENTRE DETAILS:				
7	Rent	20,000	--				
8	Rates	40,000	Description	Mach'g	Ass'y	Fin'g	Total
9	Consumables	10,000	--				
10	Power	4,750	Area sq.m	5,000	2,000	3,000	10,000
11	Cleaning	6,000	Volume cu.m	25,000	10,000	18,000	53,000
12	Light and heat	2,120	Capital vals £k	70,000	10,000	5,000	85,000
13	Maintenance	10,200	Personnel no.	10	20	5	35
14	Depreciation - Machin	8,000	Mach'y hp/hrs	8,750	350	400	9,500
15	Depreciation - Buildi	15,900	Maintenance £s	9,500	500	200	10,200
16	Indirect wages	19,600	Dep'n mach'y £s	6,500	1,000	500	8,000
17	Canteen	23,800	Consumables £s	8,000	1,000	1,000	10,000
18	Insurance - Machienry	4,250					
19	Insurance - Building	5,300					
20	Supervision	42,000					
21		----------					
22		211,920					
23		==========					
24	==						
25	L. LORD: OVERHEAD COST ANALYSIS STATEMENT						
26	--						
27		Basis of			COST CENTRES		
28	ANNUAL OVERHEADS BUDGET:	apportionment	Mach'g	Ass'y	Fin'g	Total	
29							
30			£		£	£	£	£
31	Rent	20,000 area	10,000	4,000	6,000	20,000	
32	Rates	40,000 area	20,000	8,000	12,000	40,000	
33	Consumables	10,000 (allocation)	8,000	1,000	1,000	10,000	
34	Power	4,750 hp/hrs	4,375	175	200	4,750	
35	Cleaning	6,000 area	3,000	1,200	1,800	6,000	
36	Light and heat	2,120 volume	1,000	400	720	2,120	
37	Maintenance	10,200 (allocation)	9,500	500	200	10,200	
38	Depreciation - Machin	8,000 (allocation)	6,500	1,000	500	8,000	
39	Depreciation - Buildi	15,900 volume	7,500	3,000	5,400	15,900	
40	Indirect wages	19,600 personnel	5,600	11,200	2,800	19,600	
41	Canteen	23,800 personnel	6,800	13,600	3,400	23,800	
42	Insurance - Machinery	4,250 cap. values	3,500	500	250	4,250	
43	Insurance - Building	5,300 volume	2,500	1,000	1,800	5,300	
44	Supervision	42,000 personnel	12,000	24,000	6,000	42,000	
45		----------	------------------------------------				
46		211,920	100,275	69,575	42,070	211,920	
47		==========	====================================				

Figure 12b

	A	B	C	D	E	F	G
1	L. LORD						
2	Overhead Cost Allocation and Apportionement						
3	===						
4	DATA ENTRY BLOCK						
5	---						
6	ANNUAL OVERHEADS BUDGET:£		COST CENTRE DETAILS:				
7	Rent	20,000	---				
8	Rates	40,000	Description	Mach'g	Ass'y	Fin'g	Total
9	Consumables	10,000	---				
10	Power	4,750	Area sq.m	5,000	2,000	3,000	@SUM(D10..F10)
11	Cleaning	6,000	Volume cu.m	25,000	10,000	18,000	@SUM(D11..F11)
12	Light and heat	2,120	Capital vals £k	70,000	10,000	5,000	@SUM(D12..F12)
13	Maintenance	10,200	Personnel no.	10	20	5	@SUM(D13..F13)
14	Depreciation - Machinery	8,000	Mach'y hp/hrs	8,750	350	400	@SUM(D14..F14)
15	Depreciation - Building	15,900	Maintenance £s	9,500	500	200	@SUM(D15..F15)
16	Indirect wages	19,600	Dep'n mach'y £s	6,500	1,000	500	@SUM(D16..F16)
17	Canteen	23,800	Consumables £s	8,000	1,000	1,000	@SUM(D17..F17)
18	Insurance - Machienry	4,250					
19	Insurance - Building	5,300					
20	Supervision	42,000					
21		---------------					
22		@SUM(B7..B20)					
23		===============					
24	===						
25	L. LORD: OVERHEAD COST ANALYSIS STATEMENT						
26	---						
27			Basis of		COST CENTRES		
28	ANNUAL OVERHEADS BUDGET:		apportionment	Mach'g	Ass'y	Fin'g	Total
29							
30		£		£	£	£	£
31	Rent	+B7	area	+B31/G10*D10	+B31/G10*E10	+B31/G10*F10	@SUM(D31..F31)
32	Rates	+B8	area	+B32/G10*D10	+B32/G10*E10	+B32/G10*F10	@SUM(D32..F32)
33	Consumables	+B9	(allocation)	+D17	+E17	+F17	@SUM(D33..F33)
34	Power	+B10	hp/hrs	+B34/G14*D14	+B34/G14*E14	+B34/G14*F14	@SUM(D34..F34)
35	Cleaning	+B11	area	+B35/G10*D10	+B35/G10*E10	+B35/G10*F10	@SUM(D35..F35)
36	Light and heat	+B12	volume	+B36/G11*D11	+B36/G11*E11	+B36/G11*F11	@SUM(D36..F36)
37	Maintenance	+B13	(allocation)	+D15	+E15	+F15	@SUM(D37..F37)
38	Depreciation - Machinery	+B14	(allocation)	+D16	+E16	+F16	@SUM(D38..F38)
39	Depreciation - Building	+B15	volume	+B39/G11*D11	+B39/G11*E11	+B39/G11*F11	@SUM(D39..F39)
40	Indirect wages	+B16	personnel	+B40/G13*D13	+B40/G13*E13	+B40/G13*F13	@SUM(D40..F40)
41	Canteen	+B17	personnel	+B41/G13*D13	+B41/G13*E13	+B41/G13*F13	@SUM(D41..F41)
42	Insurance - Machinery	+B18	cap. values	+B42/G12*D12	+B42/G12*E12	+B42/G12*F12	@SUM(D42..F42)
43	Insurance - Building	+B19	volume	+B43/G11*D11	+B43/G11*E11	+B43/G11*F11	@SUM(D43..F43)
44	Supervision	+B20	personnel	+B44/G13*D13	+B44/G13*E13	+B44/G13*F13	@SUM(D44..F44)
45		---------------		---			
46		@SUM(B31..B44)		@SUM(D31..D44)	@SUM(E31..E44)	@SUM(F31..F44)	@SUM(G31..G44)
47		===============		===			

144

Therefore the formula required in cell D31 reflects this:

$$B31 \times \frac{D10}{G10}$$

The formula has been entered in cell D31 as: **B31/G10*D10**

DESIGN OF THE WORKSHEET

It is probably a good idea to keep the main calculation area (A25..G47) away from the data entry area. The ranges B7..B20 and D10..F17 are the only areas where entries of data should be made. These ranges should be unprotected; the remainder of the worksheet should be protected to prevent inadvertant deletion of labels and formulae. Alteration of any figure in the unprotected ranges will result in the Overhead Cost Analysis Statement being recalculated; this is very useful if Lesley Lord decides to amend any of the original budgeted data figures.

ALTERNATIVES

Alternative appropriate bases of apportionment may be used which will give different results from those obtained in figures 12a and 12b. For example, building volume may be just as appropriate for the apportionment of rent, rates and cleaning, whereas building area could have been used for light and heat, building depreciation and building insurance.

The important aspect is to find and use a basis of apportionment most appropriate for the cost being apportioned.

[This problem is an adaptation of an example from the chapter entitled *Cost Allocation and Apportionment* in AFBIS, to which reference could be made for a more detailed explanation of the principles of cost allocation and apportionment.]

PRACTICE SESSION 13
Cost-Volume-Profit Analysis

1. Introduction

This final session is designed to provide you with some additional practice in constructing a spreadsheet to solve a management accounting problem using simple formulae.

If you have not already attempted practice session 11, please read its introduction before attempting this session. In any case, you may benefit from reading the suggested approach in that introduction again.

2. The problem

THE STIRLING BICYCLE COMPANY

The Stirling Bicycle Company are preparing their budgets for next year. They plan to produce and sell four models, ranging from the 'Aberdeen' racing bicycle to the 'Dundee' popular tourer.

(1) The Sales Director provides the following:

Model	Estimated sales demand Number of bicycles	Wholesale selling price per bicycle
Aberdeen	200	£400
Berwick	300	£300
Cairngorm	400	£200
Dundee	600	£100

(2) The budgeted variable costs of production are as follows:

Model	Parts and materials per bicycle	Labour cost per bicycle
Aberdeen	£190	£60
Berwick	£140	£40
Cairngorm	£ 90	£30
Dundee	£ 40	£20

(3) Fixed costs are budgeted at £100,000 for the year.

(4) It is expected that all models produced will be sold immediately.

146

Required:

As Assistant to the Managing Director, you are asked to prepare a Marginal Costing Statement for him, showing the contribution from each model, and the total budgeted profit for next year.

Figure 13a

	A	B	C	D	E	F	G	H
1	THE STIRLING BICYCLE COMPANY							
2	Marginal Costing Statement showing:							
3	contribution from each model & total budgeted profit for next year							
4	==							
5	Model	Sales	Variable costs per unit			Contrib'n	Prod/Sales	Total
6		price	----------------------------			per unit	(units)	Contrib'n
7			Material	Labour	Total			
8			----------------------------					
9		£	£	£	£	£		£
10								
11	Aberdeen	400	190	60	250	150	200	30,000
12	Berwick	300	140	40	180	120	300	36,000
13	Cairngorm	200	90	30	120	80	400	32,000
14	Dundee	100	40	20	60	40	600	24,000
15								---------
16					Total Contribution			122,000
17					less Fixed Costs:			100,000
18								---------
19					Budgeted Profit:			22,000
20								=========
21	==							

Figure 13b

	A	B	C	D	E	F	G	H
1	THE STIRLING BICYCLE COMPANY							
2	Marginal Costing Statement showing:							
3	contribution from each model & total budgeted profit for next year							
4	==							
5	Model	Sales	Variable costs per unit			Contrib'n	Prod/Sales	Total
6		price	----------------------------			per unit	(units)	Contrib'n
7			Material	Labour	Total			
8			----------------------------					
9		£	£	£	£	£		£
10								
11	Aberdeen	400	190	60	+C11+D11	+B11-E11	200	+F11*G11
12	Berwick	300	140	40	+C12+D12	+B12-E12	300	+F12*G12
13	Cairngorm	200	90	30	+C13+D13	+B13-E13	400	+F13*G13
14	Dundee	100	40	20	+C14+D14	+B14-E14	600	+F14*G14
15								--------------
16					Total Contribution:			@SUM(H11..H14)
17					less Fixed Costs:			100000
18								--------------
19					Budgeted Profit:			+H16-H17
20								==============
21	==							

3. The solution

Reference should be made to figures 13a and 13b.

The formulae required for the solution to this problem are simple. However, formulae should be used wherever possible, rather than calculated values; the reason for this is that, with formulae, when alternative data are substituted for the existing data, the effect on profit can be ascertained.

For example, you could see the effect on profit of producing 300 Aberdeen bicycles, instead of the present budget figure of 200, by entering 300 in cell G11. If values, based on the existing budget, had been entered in cell H11, instead of the formula multiplying F11 by G11, then the figure in cell H11 would then be incorrect and the correct revised profit figure would not show in cell H19.

Similarly, the effect of an unexpected wage increase could be reflected in revised values entered in cells D11..D14, and the correct revised budgeted profit figure would show in cell H19.

The whole worksheet should be protected, and the ranges B11..D14 and G11..G14 unprotected if revised budget entries are required.

The design of the worksheet shown in figures 13a and 13b is not necessarily the best one. The models (Aberdeen..Dundee) could be positioned horizontally at the head of columns, and the column headings (as shown in figures 13a and 13b) could be listed vertically, e.g. down column A. The important point, however, is that the Total Contribution figure should show at the end with the Fixed Costs deducted to give the Budgeted Profit (perhaps similar to the format shown in cells E16..H19).

[This problem is an example from the chapter entitled *Cost-Volume-Profit Analysis* in AFBIS, to which reference could be made for a more detailed explanation of the principles of cost-volume-profit analysis.]

APPENDIX A
Help Screens

1. Introduction

During this course of ten sessions (thirteen if you have attempted the practice sessions), you have gained experience of the basics of worksheet creation and design. You have also obtained glimpses of some of the powerful potential of spreadsheets. On your way, you have used or seen a few of the following:

Movement keys	e.g. <Home> in READY mode to return to cell A1
Function keys	e.g <F5> for GoTo
Mode Indicators	e.g. READY
Statistical Functions	e.g. @SUM
Financial Functions	e.g @PV
Date Functions	e.g. @DATE
Logical Functions	e.g. @IF
Macro keystrokes	e.g. {UP}

There are, of course, many more keystrokes, indicators and functions under each of the above headings which you may want to use in your future spreadsheet explorations.

How to find them and learn how to use them?

There are two approaches:

(1) Refer to the excellent manuals that came with your program. In particular, practise using the table of contents and the index to find what you want and, most important, try it out on a worksheet. (Save the worksheet before you experiment.)

(2) Use the Help Screens which are lurking behind your screen, ready to spring into life if only you will let them. Many students spend valuable time desperately trying to find somebody to help them solve a problem when the answer is only a few keystrokes away.

Each program has its own helpscreen system. In the following paragraphs, you will learn how to use the system appropriate to your particular program.

Paragraph 2 for Lotus 1-2-3 Release 2.0

Paragraph 3 for Lotus 1-2-3 Release 2.2

Paragraph 4 for VP-Planner and VP-Planner PLUS

Paragraph 5 for As-Easy-As

For practice, you will suppose that you want to remember what the financial function @PV does and how to enter it.

At the same time you will get the feel of moving round the help screens.

Load a blank (or any other saved worksheet), check that you are in READY mode, and carry out the following:

2. Help screens {123} Release 2.0

Press | <F1> |

A screen replaces your worksheet (temporarily), and tells you about READY mode, which is the mode you were in when you asked for Help.

Press | <End> |

The cursor moves to *How to Use Help* in the bottom right-hand corner of the screen.

Press | <Enter> |

This screen tells you how to use the Help Facility. Read it and try out pressing <End> and <Home>.

Move the cursor to *Help Index*.

Press | <Enter> |

You are now at the Help Index screen. You are looking for help with an @ function, so

Move the cursor to *@Functions*.

Press | <Enter> |

Read the screen about @Functions. Since PV (Present Value) is a Financial function,

Move the cursor to *Financial*.

Press | <Enter> |

A screen appears with details of various financial functions, but @PV is not one of them. However, the cursor is over the word *Continued*, so

Press | <Enter> | and details of @PV appear to refresh your memory.

Press | <Esc> | to return to your worksheet.

150

Now you have made a preliminary skirmish into help screens, why not get some practice in using them by simply pressing <F1> and exploring?

When you have finished, please read paragraph 6 below.

3. Help screens {123} Release 2.2

Press | <F1> |

A screen replaces your worksheet (temorarily), and is the Lotus 1-2-3 Help Index. The cursor should be on *About 1-2-3 Help.*

Press | <Enter> |

This screen tells you how to use the Help Facility. Read it and try out pressing <End> and <Home>.

Move the cursor to *Help Index.*

Press | <Enter> |

You are now at the Help Index screen. You are looking for help with an @ function, so

Move the cursor to *@Function Index.*

Press | <Enter> |

An @Function Index screen appears. However, @PV is not listed. However, move the cursor to the word *Continued* at the foot of the screen, and

Press | <Enter> |

@PV is in the second column. Move the cursor there and press <Enter>

Details of @PV appear to refresh your memory.

Press | <Esc> | to return to your worksheet.

Now you have made a preliminary skirmish into help screens, why not get some practice in using them by simply pressing <F1> and exploring?

When you have finished, please read paragraph 6 below.

4. Help screens {VP} and {VPP}

Press | <F1> |

A screen replaces your worksheet (temporarily), and tells you about *Using Help*. Read this screen, and then

Press | <F1> | again.

You are now at the Help Index screen. You are looking for help with a Financial Function, which is page 18; so

Press | <F5> | Type | 18 | <Enter>

Details of @PV appear to refresh your memory.

Press | <Esc> | to return to your worksheet.

Now you have made a preliminary skirmish into help screens, why not get some practice in using them by simply pressing <F1> and exploring?

When you have finished, please read paragraph 6 below.

5. Help screens {AEA}

Press | <F1> |

A screen replaces your worksheet (temporarily), which is an index of the help screens.

You are looking for an @Financial function. You can either press the down arrow until you come to it, or

Press | <Shift> + @ |

The cursor moves down to @Date/Time.

Press | <d> | to highlight @Finance.

You will see the window to the right displaying FINANCIAL FUNCTIONS.

Press | <a> | to move the cursor to the heading FINANCIAL FUNCTIONS.

Press | <PgDn> | three times

and details of @PV appear to refresh your memory.

Press | <Esc> | to return to your worksheet.

Now you have made a preliminary skirmish into help screens, why not get some practice in using them by simply pressing <F1> and exploring?

When you have finished, please read paragraph 6 below.

6. Menu maps

Some students find "maps" of the menu system useful, particularly in the early stages of acquaintance with spreadsheets.

Lotus 1-2-3 Help Facility covers all the commands under the topic *1-2-3 Commands* and *Command Menus* (1-2-3 Main Menu in release 2.2) in the Help Index. The manual has

APPENDIX B

Menu Map
for 1-2-3 and VP-Planner Plus

LOTUS 1-2-3 (R 2.0) and VP-PLANNER PLUS

[Note for As-Easy-As users: A separate abbreviated menu map is provided in Appendix C.]

Some students find "maps" of the menu system useful, particularly in the early stages of acquaintance with spreadsheets.

Lotus 1-2-3 Help Facility covers all the commands under the topic *1-2-3 Commands* and *Command Menus (1-2-3 Main Menu* in release 2.2) in the Help Index. The manual has individual menu maps, e.g. in *Quick Reference* and at the start of Chapter 12 for Worksheet Commands in the Reference Manual (Release 2.2). However, there is no "at-a-glance" chart showing an overall annotated view, and this is provided in this appendix.

VP-Planner Help Facility covers all the commands under screens 30-49 in the Help Index. The screen numbers in VP-Planner Plus are arranged differently. The VP-Planner Plus manual has individual menu charts at the start of each section under Command Reference. However, there is no "at-a-glance" chart showing an overall annotated view, and this is provided in Appendix B.

Menu maps such this are small-scale maps, help screens are medium-scale maps, and the manuals are large-scale maps. Each type is suitable for its own particlar purpose. For exploring the hills, small-scale maps are useless and can be dangerous.

This menu-map is designed to help you find your way around the menu structure of 123 and VPP. It is not a complete map of either program's menus; selections have been made of the most useful menu items.

If you look at the complete menu maps in the program manuals, you will see that some menus descend through many levels; for example, in 123,

/Worksheet, Global, Default, Other, International, Date, A (MM/DD/YY)

The lower levels are mainly self-explanatory, though you would be well advised to look up the manual for guidance; you will also learn more thoroughly by doing so.

Tip 1: You may find it helpful to consult the help screens. Press <F1> and follow the instructions on the screen. See Appendix A on how to use the help screens.

Tip 2: As you press each menu command, look for and read the explanation or list of submenus on the screen in the control panel or drop-down menu.

Tip 3: The index at the end of this book shows key sequences, where appropriate, against the entry, as well as referring you to the session and paragraph number where further guidance is given.

MENU MAP

/ WORKSHEET

Global	Controls overall worksheet settings
Format	Sets standard for numeric displays
Fixed	Fixed number of decimal places
Scientific	Exponential format
Currency	Currency format e.g £1,000.00
, (Comma)	Comma format e.g 1,000.00
General	Standard format e.g 1000.00
+/-	Horizontal bar graph
Percent	Percent format e.g 1.00%
Date	Date and time formats; various options
Text	Displays formulae
Label-Prefix	Choice of alignments
Column-Width	Sets global column-width for entire worksheet
Recalculation	Various options: Natural, Columnwise, Rowwise, Automatic, Manual, Iteration
Protection	Choices: Enable, Disable
Default	Establishes initial (default) printer, disk and display settings.
	{123} has choices for Printer, Directory, Status, Update, and "Other": International (including currency sign), Help, Clock
	{VPP} displays a screen where all the choices can be seen, and includes Printer, Directory, External-path, Hardware, Custom, Status, Update and Other.
Insert	Inserts blank Columns or Rows
Delete	Deletes Columns or Rows
Column	Changes width of current column
	Includes Set, Reset and {123} Hide and Display
Erase	Erases the entire worksheet from memory
	Prompt: Yes or No
Titles	Freezes rows and columns above and to the left of the cell pointer
	Choices: Both, Horizontal, Vertical, Clear

Window	Controls split screen and synchronized scrolling Choices: Horizontal, Vertical,Sync, Unsync, Clear
Status	Displays current settings
Page	Inserts a row containing a page-break symbol above the cell pointer

/ RANGE

Format	See under /Worksheet, Global, Format above Also: Reset and Hide (Hidden)
Label	Changes alignment for a label or range of labels
Erase	Erases a cell or range of cells
Name	
Create	Creates or changes a range name
Delete	Deletes a range name
Labels	Creates range names from a range of labels
Reset	Deletes all range names
Table	Creates a table of range names
Justify	Reformats a column of label cells
Protect	Prevents changes to a range of cells
Unprotect	Unprotects globally protected cells
Input	Limits cursor movement to unprotected cells

/ COPY	Copies a cell or range of cells
/ MOVE	Moves a cell or range of cells

/ FILE

Retrieve	Erases the current worksheet from memory and loads a file from disk
Save	Saves the entire worksheet in a worksheet file Choices: Cancel, Replace, Backup
Combine	Incorporates all or part of a worksheet file into the current worksheet Choices: Copy, Add, Subtract
Xtract	Saves a range of cells in a worksheet file Choices: Formulas, Values
Erase	Erases a file from disk Choices: Worksheet, Print, Graph, Other
List	Lists files in current directory Choices: Worksheet, Print, Graph, Other
Import	Superimposes print file on current file at cursor position Choices: Text, Numbers

Directory   Displays or resets the current directory

/ PRINT   Prints current worksheet or stores it in a text file

File   Stores current worksheet in a text file

                            Enter file name; then choices as for Printer

Printer   Prints current worksheet

    Range   Defines cells to be printed

    Line   Advances paper by one line

    Page   Advances paper to top of next page

    Options

        Header   Text line at top of each page

        Footer   Text line at bottom of each page

        Margins   Set margins, Left, Right, Top, Bottom

        Borders   Columns (left)/Rows (top) for each page

        Set-up   String e.g. \027\015 for condensed print

                         Leave blank if printer controlled

        Page-length Lines per page: e.g. 66 (11″), 70 (A4)

        Other

            As-displayed   Prints as displayed on screen

            Cell-Formulas One cell per line; prints control panel display
                                for each cell

            Formatted   Standard printing including Options

            Unformatted   Does not print Options

      {VP} Page#   Prints page number at top right-hand corner

      {VP} No-Page# Turns off Page#
                        [Note: Page numbers can be included in headers
                        and footers {123}{VP}.]

      {VP} R/C#s   Prints row and column references (numbers and letters)
                        as shown by most of Figures in this book

      {VP} Stop-R/C#s Turns off R/C#s

      {VP} Background Printing On/Off

      {VP} Wide-print Sideways printing On/Off

    Clear   Cancels choice of print settings

                            Choices: All, Range, Borders, Format

    Align   Tells program that printer is at top of page

Go	Prints worksheet as instructed in settings
Quit	Returns to READY mode

/ GRAPH

Type	Selects type of graph Choices: Line, Bar, XY, Stacked-bar, Pie
X	Sets range of cells for horizontal axis (slice for Pie)
A, B, C, D, E, F	Sets up to six (A..F) ranges for vertical axis
Reset	Cancels all or individual range settings Choices: Graph X A B C D E F Quit
View	Displays current graph
Print {VP}	Prints current graph on a graphics printer [{123} prints using Printgraph program]
Save	Saves graph as a .PIC file
Options	
Legend	Defines legends for symbols or patterns Choices: A..F
Format	Specifies way lines drawn in line or XY graph Choices: Graph, A B C D E F Choices: Lines, Symbols, Both, Neither
Titles	Specifies titles for: Choices: First, Second, X-axis, Y-axis
Grid	Include or exclude grid lines (not for pie graphs) Choices: Horizontal, Vertical, Both, Clear
Scale	Sets scales on X and Y axes Choices: Y-scale, X-scale, Skip Choices: Automatic, Manual, Lower, Upper, Format, Indicator (Format has choices: see under /WGF or /RF)
Colour	Displays graph in colour; see manual for details
B&W	Displays in Black and White; see manual for details
Data-Labels	Uses contents of a range as labels; for example values may be printed at top of bars Choices: A B C D E F Choices: Centre, Left, Above, Right, Below
Quit	Returns to the Graph menu
Name	Performs the following:
Use	Makes a previously named graph the current graph
Create	Names the current graph with current settings
Delete	Deletes a named graph

Reset	Deletes all named graphs

/ DATA

Fill	Fills a range with a sequence of values, equally spaced, top to bottom, left to right
Table	Performs sensitivity (What if?) analyses Choices: 1-variable, 2-variable, Reset
Sort	Arranges data in specified order
Data-range	Specifies range to be sorted
Primary-key	Specifies first field to sort
Secondary-key	Specifies second field to sort
Reset	Clears data-range and sort keys
Go	Carries out the specified sort
Quit	Returns to READY mode
Query	Locates and edits selected records
Input	Specifies range of records to search
Criterion	Specifies criteria range for selection criteria
Output	Specifies range to which selected records are copied
Find	Highlights selected records in input range
Extract	Copies selected records to specified output range
Unique	As Extract, omitting duplicate records
Delete	Deletes selected records from input range
Reset	Clears input, criterion and output ranges
Quit	Returns to READY mode
Distribution	Calculates frequency distribution of specified range of values

[Note: {VP}{VPP}{123} have additional (different) Data commands]

/ TOOLS {VPP}	For details, see manual
/ SYSTEM	Leave program temporarily to run a DOS program Caution: Save your worksheet first before using this command Refer to your manual for details To return to program, type at DOS prompt: exit<return>
/ QUIT	Quits the spreadsheet program

APPENDIX C

Menu Map
for As-Easy-As (version 4.00Q)

AS-EASY-AS (Version 4.00Q)

Some students find "maps" of the menu system useful, particularly in the early stages of acquaintance with spreadsheets. This menu-map is designed to help you find your way around the menu structure.

There are useful menu maps in the program's 'Help' facility which can be accessed using the <F1> Help key. Choose the topic you want, and press <→> to move to the window; scroll if needed, using the keys indicated at the foot of the screen. See Appendix A for further details.

This As-Easy-As Help Facility has separate windows e.g. for Worksheet commands under ComWSheet which show clear individual menu maps. The manual has a detailed Menu Command Summary section. However, there is no "at-a-glance" chart showing an overall view, and this is provided by this Appendix.

Menu maps such as this are small-scale maps, help screens are medium-scale maps, and the manuals are large-scale maps. Each type is suitable for its own particular purpose. For exploring the hills, small scale maps are useless and can be dangerous.

Tip 1: You may find it helpful to consult the help screens. Press <F1> and follow the instructions on the screen. See Appendix A on how to use the help screens.

Tip 2: As you press each menu command, look for and read the explanation or list of sub-menus on the screen in the control panel or drop-down menu.

Tip 3: The index at the end of this book shows key sequences, where appropriate, against the entry, as well as referring you to the session and paragraph number where further guidance is given.

/ WORKSHEET

ColWidth	Set / Reset	
Delete	Column / Row	
Erase	No/Yes	
Border	Horizon / Vertical / Both / Suppress / Clear	
Insert	Column / Row / Page	
General	Format	Fixed / Science / , (comma) / Currency / General / Date: (various choices) / Percent / +/- / Text / Hide / Reset

Label	Left / Right / Centre
Column	
Recalc	Manual / Auto
Protect	Enable / Disable
Zeros	No / Yes
Negative	No / Yes

INSTALL	Colors	Text / MenuBk / MenuFr / Csr / Ptr / Bord / Bot / Top / Neg / UnPr / Quit
	Punctuate	Decimal / Argument / Currency / Thousand / MenuKey / Quit
	Dimension	
	Ega43	
	Addin	Create / Delete / Reset
	SAVE	
	Quit	

Macro	Compose / Execute / Step / Quit
Summary	
Window	Horizon / Vertical / Sync / UnSync / Clear
Text	Find / Replace / Justify / Word

/ RANGE

Audit	Trace / CrossRef / OverView / Quit
Copy	Value / Transpose / Scale / Invert
Erase	
Format	Fixed / Science / , (comma) / Currency / General / / Date (various choices) / Percent / +/- / Text / Hide / Reset
Lock	Yes / No
Name	Create / Delete / Reset / Table / Build
Prefix	Left / Center / Right
Quit	

/ COPYCELL

/ MOVECELL

/ ARRAY

Add / Subtract / Multiply / Invert / Transpose / E-Solve / Quit

/DATA

Fill	
Parse	
Question	InpRange / OutRange / Criteria / FindRec / Extract / Reset / Quit
Sort	D-Range / P(1)-key / S(2)-key / Reset / Go / Quit
Table	1-Column / 2-Column

GoalSeek	Input / Output / Desire / Quit
Regress	XData / Ydata / Output / Quit
Bin	
Input	Form / Criteria / Range / Quit

/ FILE

Retrieve	
Store	Cancel / Replace / Backup
Merge	All / Range
	↓ ↓
	Value / Formula
	↓ ↓
	Replace / Sum / Diff
Xport	Wks / DbIII
Import	Values / Text / DbIII / List
Erase	W?? / P?? / Other
List	W?? / P?? / Other
Dir	
UpLink	
Option	

/ GRAPHICS

Type	X-Y / Bar / Pie / Stack / Line / Cume / Hloc / Radar / Area / Delta
X A..F	
Labels	A / B / C / D / E / F / Reset
Options	Legend:	A / B / C / D / E / F / Line / Table / None
	Format:	Graph / A / B / C / D / E / F
		↓ ↓ ↓ ↓ ↓ ↓
		None / Line / Symbols / Both / Depth
	Titles:	First / Second / X / Y / Quit
	Scale:	X-Scale / Y-Scale / Quit
		↓ ↓
		Auto / Manual / Upper / Lower /
		/ Format (usual choices) / Step / Exp / Normal / Quit
	Grid	Horizon / Vertical / Both / Clear / Dot / Solid
	Color	No / Yes
	Quit	
Reset	Graph / X / A / B / C / D / E / F
Name	Use / Create / Delete / Merge / Split / Reset
View	
Plot	Image:	High / Wide / Top / Bottom / Left / Quit
	Density	Low / High

Hardware	PIC / LASER / FX/MX / 24-PIN	
Paper	Height / Width / Quit	
Orient	Portrait / Landscape	
Eject		
GO		
Quit		

Quit

/ PRINTTO

Printer	Range		
	Border:	Rows / Columns / None	
	LineFeed		
	PageAdv		
	Options	Margins:	Left / Right / PgLen / Top / Bot
		Setup	
		PgLength	
		Header	
		Footer	
		Type:	As-Seen / Contents / NoForm
		Quit	
	Adjust		
	Go		
	Quit		

File
Append

/ USER

Shell   Leave program temporarily to run a DOS program
               Caution: Save your worksheet first before using this command
               Refer to your manual for details
               To return to program, type at DOS prompt: exit<return>
LndScape   [Executable AddIn]
               Range / LineFeed / PageAdv / Option (Margin / LineSpace / CharSpace /
               / Pglength / Width / SkipPerf / Quit) / Type (Expanded / Normal /
               / Condensed) / Go / Quit

/ EXIT

OBJECTIVE TESTS
Answers

Question Numbers:

	1	2	3	4	5	6	7	8	9	10
SESSION:										
1	C	B	D	C	D	D	A	B	A	A
2	B	A	A	B	C	D	B	B	D*	A
3	B	A	D	C	B	D	B	A	D	A
4	C	B	A	D	C	B	A	A	B	C
5	D	C	B	D	A	B	C	D	D	A
6	C	C	C	C	A	D	A	C	A	B
7	A	D	C	A	C	B	A	C	A	C
8	C	D	A	B	B	D	B	A	D	D
9	B	A	C	D	C	A	D	B	C	C
10	A	B	D	A	C	A	D	D	C	D

*C{VPP}

INDEX

Index